GW00818517

IT COSTS, A BOMB

HOW MILLIONS WERE LOST GOING OVER THE TOP... ALL IN A GOOD CAUSE

John Reed

HAWKSMERE

© John Reed 1989

Published by Hawksmere Ltd
12–18 Grosvenor Gardens
London SW1W 0DH

British Library Cataloguing in Publication Data
Reed, John
It costs, a bomb: how millions were lost
going over the top, all in a good cause.
1. Great Britain. Military equipment. Supply and demand
I. Title
338.4'3623

ISBN 1-85418-060-6

Production in association with
Book Production Consultants
47 Norfolk Street, Cambridge

Typeset by
KeyStar, St Ives, Cambridge

Printed in Great Britain by
Bookcraft (Bath) Ltd,
Midsomer Norton, Avon

CONTENTS

INTRODUCTION

This book aims to provide a lighthearted view of the costly misfortunes which all too frequently overtake very expensive defence equipment programmes – all of which have been conceived in a good cause.

It is certainly not intended as an in-depth study of either defence equipment or the defence industry. Nor does it attempt to draw conclusions about the reasons for the mistakes beyond the inescapable fact that a very large **System** is at work grinding on so remorselessly that it is almost impossible to apply a brake or change it into reverse gear. It is **The System** that is the 'villain of the piece' rather than individuals. If the book has a hero it's the luckless tax-payer who time and time again has had to pick up the bill for the things that have gone so badly wrong.

It was perhaps appropriate that on the day that I was to discuss our plans for this book I paused on a walk to Westminster to watch a ceremonial parade by a Guards battalion. Later that morning I sat at the Press table in a House of Commons committee room as the Select Committee of Defence heard evidence on why it was that a newly developed missile system was still unable to distinguish between friendly and enemy aircraft. In the afternoon I talked with my publishers about our ideas for a book which highlighted the ridiculous and wasteful situations which often – too often – arise when governments have tried to balance threats to the nation's security with scarce resources.

These were situations far removed from the guardsmen who had paraded for a visiting dignitary on Horseguards Parade earlier on that unusually hot day. The precision with which their red and black ranks formed and wheeled was the outward sign of a centuries-old tradition of dedication that it would be impertinent to deride.

It would be equally unworthy deliberately to seek out the ridiculous – although ridiculous there certainly has been – in the efforts of the many thousands of individual civil servants by whose efforts Britain's armed forces have been sustained through the years.

This book is not about such people. It is about **The System**, the balancing of resources and the effort to retain the position on the frontiers of the technology that is necessary for the nation's defence.

The System has on occasions responded magnificently. For the most part, though, it is fallible, like those other **Systems** which can mistakenly add a thousand pounds to our domestic gas bill or for all their sophistication have to confess that 'the lady who writes the cheques is on holiday' whenever we are owed money.

Defence is, to use a trendy expression, a *megabusiness*. Politicians love to talk about it but don't always know exactly what it is that they are talking about. Civil servants can make good careers for themselves by opening and closing the purse strings at the right moment. Industry – a term which might or might not embrace a multitude of sins – would dearly like to make big profits out of it. Like most other activities dominated by all-powerful **Systems** defence tries to keep its mistakes hidden from public view. To do so it often has to resort to the use of half truths or worse. It probably has good reasons for doing so but its determination not to be caught out makes the pursuit of its cock-ups all the more enjoyable. It is tempting for an author to try to draw all manner of conclusions about managerial processes from the way in which systems perform, but those very systems which decide which equipment will eventually reach our armed forces are unique in their scale and complexity. It is better by far for the reader to draw his or her own conclusions – but not to forget that every penny (new or old) has been spent in the sincere belief that it was all in a good cause!

St Austell, Cornwall   July 1989

RIGHT OR WRONG – STAND STILL!

The trouble with defence is that it is so terribly complicated that a state-of-the-art weapon can work in theory, but in practice can leave its users more concerned about the state of a part.

Picture the scene. It is nearly twelve hours since the battle began with tracked amphibians crawling out of the Mediterranean Sea up the beach and carrying the infantry across the promenade into the town to link up with the parachutists who landed a day earlier. More soldiers have joined them and the day's fighting has gone their way. Like all soldiers since time immemorial they are waiting for supplies, rations and ammunition – but most of all they need transport. Today's army, like Napoleon's, might still march on its stomach but it needs wheels. In the harbour a newly-arrived landing craft opens its massive bow doors and lowers the ramp along which the first of the much needed trucks will disembark.

The first of the green-painted trucks rolls ashore. Does it bring ammunition? Or rations? No such luck. It is an officers' mess truck carrying the regimental silver belonging to a distinguished cavalry regiment which was withdrawn from the order of battle some months ago and is currently still safely in its barracks not far from London.

Keen observers of the military scene might be quick to point out that if this scenario was enacted in the Mediterranean, why were the vehicles green? Should they not have been painted a stone or sand colour? Of course they should have been. Unfortunately the supply of stone-coloured paint was despatched from England deep in the hold of a cargo ship and could not be unloaded at the time it was required several weeks earlier.

That incident actually occurred during the 1956 Anglo-French landings at Port Said. Twenty-six years later as the British fleet steamed southwards to do battle in the Falklands the grim truth dawned that it was still every bit as difficult to get the right thing into the right place at the right time. On that occasion it was possible to solve many of the day-to-day problems by throwing money at them in various ways. Nevertheless at the end of the campaign there was no shortage of people prepared to swear that real life was nothing like the textbooks and manoeuvres had told them it should be.

The trouble with defence is that it is so terribly complicated. It is not just a question of knowing what you need to beat your enemy – or even of making sure that it's where you want it to be when you want it to be there. You've got to be sure that it'll do most of what you wanted it to do, and that your enemy doesn't know about the things that you hoped it could do but which have thus far proved to be beyond the wit of man. The worst possible thing that you can do is actually to use the equipment in anger, because then he'll know precisely what it can't do.

Our government spends a lot of our money – about £20 billion each year – in the good cause of our defence against those who it considers to be our enemies. A lot of that money simply goes down the drain. Sometimes that is because inefficiencies can never be entirely eliminated from a big organisation – and our defence establishment is a very big organisation. Sometimes it's because for all its gruff bemedalled exterior it can act as if it is chasing moonbeams.

■

Talking to the Back Room Boys

Consider what can happen when a senior service officer finds that the bad guys have got a submarine that can dive deeper than ours or that they possess some new-fangled electronic warfare system that could create mayhem with his communications systems. He goes through to the back room and asks the scientists what they can do about it.

> *'Gee whizz. Do you really mean that you will be able to do all that?' he asks incredulously when they've finished.*

> *'Not right now,' they reply, 'but we can't really do all that we know about now for a few years yet anyhow – and by that time we should have some other good ideas just about coming to the boil – so why not ask for them too?'*

> *He asks ... and then things begin to go wrong.*

> *There might not be enough money to do the research at the right time.*

> *The good ideas might be a little less good than the scientists thought.*

> *The likelihood is that at some stage the service chiefs are going to ask 'Will it be ready when you said it would?'*

> *The reply will probably be 'Not unless you spend some more money on it'.*

This puts the serviceman in a spot. He doesn't have any money. The money belongs to the civil servants. Ever the simple soldier he remembers his earliest days in uniform. Then if he put a foot out of line he had no chance to retract it. *Right or Wrong Stand Still* – a barked command from the drill instructor that sticks in the memory and says all that needs to be said.

■

The Threat

For all that, though, the serviceman does have one trump card. He knows about **The Threat**. How he knows about it and whether what he says he knows is entirely accurate is sometimes open to argument. It is not so long ago that virtually the entire United States military establishment believed the Soviets had a new super-tank. Eventually it emerged that such a tank was not actually in production and indeed it might be a year or two before it saw the light of day. That didn't worry the soldiers too much. Real or not it was **The Threat** and they needed money to confront it. Unless they got their bids for money in quickly enough they would be left without any suitable answer to the tank when it eventually rolled out of the factory.

For much the same reasons there are always voices to be heard protesting that such-and-such a weapon does not work well enough. The truth may be different. It can work well enough today but may not be so much use in a few years' time. So the rule is if you want to be sure that you've got something good enough to meet **The Threat** in a few years' time, the sooner you start rubbishing to-day's hardware the better your chances of getting the necessary money. The more machiavellian mind might see this approach as offering a bonus in so far as you've got your enemy guessing about the good (or bad) shape of your armoury. The problem is that you also run the risk of leaving your own side – which includes the people with the money – in much the same confused state.

■

Challenging Challenger

Take the case of the British Army's Main Battle Tanks. Historically the defence establishment had spent a great deal of time and energy arguing over whether it should have medium-sized cruiser or heavier infantry tanks. So in the late 1940s it came up with a neat compromise by calling the Centurion tank – which came closer to the tankman's ideal than some of its predecessors – a Heavy Cruiser Tank. Centurion was by any standards a good tank, but its successor Chieftain, which came into production in the 1960s, was less well received. The consensus view was that it had a fairly good gun but an engine that was at first far from satisfactory. By the time the engine had been beefed-up, the gun turret was beginning to look a little aged, but in the meantime the government had won an order from the late Shah of Iran for a tank called Shir, which was essentially a Chieftain with a better engine and transmission and better performance, which meant a more stable firing platform for the gun.

At the same time the Ministry of Defence was pushing ahead with plans for a new Main Battle Tank known as MBT80. Arguably it ought to have known that there is no surer recipe for problems than giving a project a name which implies the expectation that it will see service at a certain time. 'Bridging for the Eighties' was an engineering project which eventually had to be re-named 'Bridging for the Nineties' when it fell far behind the expectations of its original sponsors, and so it was with MBT80.

By 1980 the MBT80 programme had got so far behind that it seemed unlikely to enter service before the early 1990s. Dame Fortune took a hand when the Shah was deposed and his successors decided that they did not want Shir. The answer was simple. Cancel MBT80, re-name Shir as Challenger and make a few relatively inexpensive changes to bring it into line with British Army needs. Moreover with much of the development already done the first order for 243 tanks would cost the tax-payer only £300 million and bring an end to the costly years of development that were still necessary for MBT80.

The original plan was to buy less Challengers than there were Chieftains in service and to develop another tank to replace the Chieftains that would still be soldiering on after the last of the Challengers had been delivered. When the men from the ministry decided to call this new tank the MBT2000 the cynics were heard muttering that by opting for the millenium rather than a decade at least they might have neatly side-stepped the need for a name change when the project fell behind schedule – which of course it did.

When the British Army got its first Challengers in 1983–4 it quickly ran into problems. Not the least of these was the fact that the British were soundly beaten into a lowly place in an annual NATO Canadian Army tank gunnery competition. Challenger's gun system was showing its age. At first the soldiers put on a bold face and replied in much the same way as England's cricket selectors do after yet another defeat at the hand of the West Indies. 'It's rather like comparing apples with oranges,' they told their critics. 'These fellows spend all year practising for the competition. We just send along some of our chaps after a few weeks' training – so we did jolly well all things considered.' But beneath their bluff exteriors the soldiers were worried. Challenger would not be a match for **The Threat** in the 1990s.

What did they do? Of course they went to the people with the money and asked if they could buy the American M-1 Abrams tank. After all they knew that its gun worked – it had beaten them in the competition. It seems that at first the men with the money rather liked the idea. The American tank was cheaper and would be what they like to call an *off-the-shelf buy* – something that has already been developed at somebody else's expense and is ready and waiting to do the job that you have in mind. However one of the groups who we haven't discussed yet remained unconvinced by the apparent logic of buying the Abrams tank. It was the majority of the ten thousand or so companies who make up Britain's defence industry, led on this occasion not surprisingly by the people who hoped to build still more Challengers.

Their protests proved to be made of the very stuff on which politicians, the press and television thrive. Buy American and the once great industry that had built Challenger and Chieftain would slip into oblivion taking the jobs of thousands with it. We'll hear much more about the mayhem that such arguments can cause, but the upshot was that the tank makers got another chance. Whilst they were bent over their drawing boards – or to put it more precisely staring into their computer terminals – things were going adrift elsewhere on the battlefield.

■
A LAW unto Itself

One of the more bizarre foul-ups concerned a handy little anti-tank missile known as LAW80. There were high hopes of LAW80 when it was selected as the Army's Light Anti-Armour Weapon. The answer to the foot soldier's dream it was small enough to be carried by one man and was supposed to be able to blast its way through up to 600 mm of armour. That should have given it a punch big enough to stop any tank that the planners could see coming off the drawing boards, and indeed to give its designers their due it made effective use of some very advanced warhead technology. At the time at which it was being touted around the corridors of power LAW80 was what defence people like to call *state of the art* – it's their way of saying 'it's about as far as we can get at the moment'. The trouble with LAW80 was that even as the programme to develop it got under way the Soviet Army was looking at new ways to keep its tanks intact.

That was in 1978, and the Ministry of Defence on its own admission took a little time to grasp the significance of what was happening on the other side. When it did it was a classic *Right or Wrong Stand Still* situation. The contracts had been placed. It believed that it could muddle through somehow, and it was not until 1980 that it realised that it was in such deep trouble that its contractors would be unable to meet the requirement. Even then all concerned soldiered on manfully in the vain hope of a breakthrough in just about every sense of the word. None came. The experts seem to have been firm believers in the principle that 'where there's life there's hope' except that by 'life' they really meant 'money' – and the money didn't run out until the end of 1984, by which time the weapon should have been in service anyhow. In the meantime the ministry decided to stop chasing moonbeams and to go ahead with production. There was the usual ballyhoo, with gushing press releases, and a £200 million production contract for LAW80's developers Hunting Engineering.

What the ministry did not say though was that it had known for at least a couple of years that it was out of its depth. Four years later in 1989 Hunting had delivered as many as 14,000 LAW80s, but the early muddles, the vain search for the big breakthrough, and lesser problems with the rocket's motor and even with the spotting rifle which the soldier uses to mark his target, had taken their toll. The defence community has its own neat turn of phrase to describe such disasters. *Slippage*, although not an elegant word, suggests a rather graceful descent into serious delay.

By 1989 LAW80 had 'slipped' by five years and cost the British tax-payer a cool £43 million more than had originally been planned.

However that was not the whole story. In the meantime the *state of the art* had moved on to such an extent that the Russians now had something called *reactive armour*, a system of boxes containing thin strips of flat explosive which can be fixed to the vulnerable parts of a tank or armoured personnel carrier. If these are hit by the traditional infantry anti-tank projectile they detonate it sufficiently prematurely to prevent the hull being penetrated. It wasn't even high technology and the savants were quick to form the view that it would not be long before nearly every army followed suit. If all that was being said was to be believed LAW80 could finish up as a very expensive way to blow up a lorry.

Keeping in Touch – That'll do Nicely

The military man tends to look at such untidy muddles, nod wisely and make some remark to the effect that 'that's the nature of the business we're in I'm afraid. It's rotten luck on a chap when the other fellow does something like that – and after all everybody knows that foreigners cheat.'

Of course the problem is that even the simplest idea takes time to be translated into practice. When you have to drag it through the corridors and in and out of the committee rooms which make up so much of government the chances that it will be overtaken by the course of events become all the greater.

The United States Army needed a new radio set for its Special Forces. These are the hard men who slide down ropes, kick in embassy windows, climb cliffs and creep around in the dark. The last thing that they want is equipment which is likely to get in the way as they go about their business. It took several years to come up with what the committees decided was the right design for their new radio. During that time our old friend the *state of the art* moved along and the soldiers eventually got a radio set weighing 45 lbs at a time when more efficient equipment weighing less than 5 lbs was beginning to come off the drawing board. But even their troubles were slight in comparison with those which fell upon the communications specialists at their headquarters. They had ordered a mobile base station in 1978 and waited patiently until 1985 for delivery.

They got a piece of equipment (AN/TSC-99) which was too large to be moved on European roads without a special permit and which early in its service career failed on average every 5.6 hours – they had asked for an average of 1200 hours between failures.

No doubt the Americans had waited so long for their radio equipment that even that which they got was welcome. Eighteen months before, in the course of their landings on Granada, one of their number had been obliged to use his credit card to call his base in North Carolina and ask a colleague there to relay a request to a warship lying off the beach on which he had been put ashore to provide his unit with covering fire. Their predicament would have been familiar to observers of the defence scene.

Quite simply, the longer a requirement remains unfulfilled the more it becomes distorted. Far from the battlefield on which the fate of soldiers hung on their commanding officer having paid his American Express account for the previous month, Britain's Ministry of Defence decided that by spending £4 million on a new Private Automatic Branch telephone exchange it could save itself some money. Unfortunately it did not have enough people to oversee the project and by the time that it was able to implement the scheme it had managed to spend an additional £16 million on rented equipment.

The time has now come for us to look at some of the reasons why it takes so long to get a particular piece of equipment into service.

2

'THE SYSTEM'
A PLACE
FOR EVERYTHING
AND EVERYTHING
IN ITS PLACE

Who takes these decisions which no matter how well-intentioned so often disappoint the user and cost the tax-payer more than he had bargained for?

Everything begins with **The Threat**. The services and their Defence Intelligence Staff keep **The Threat** under review, comparing it to the equipment that they have available. Naturally the servicemen want the newest the shiniest and the best and see their equipment in terms of *service life*. The theory is that a piece of equipment is going to last them for a certain number of years and that at a certain point in its life the service chiefs will ask their Operational Requirements staff to devise what is known as a *Staff Target* based on their assessment of **The Threat** at the time at which the equipment it envisages is likely to enter service.

So there we are right at the beginning of the process with a very big question mark over what will actually be needed. As we have already seen with LAW80 things can go dreadfully wrong.

∎

The Long Journey
Through the Corridors
of Power

The *Staff Target* passes into the hands of the committees, one of which, the EQUIPMENT POLICY COMMITTEE, will already have been watching over major projects just to make sure that nobody has been overambitious. The EPC controls a number of lesser committees which oversee projects as they evolve from their *Staff Target* origins via a feasibility study – which is really not much to do with technical feasibility and rather more to do with winning friends for the project and making sure that there is going to be enough money available for it – and a STAFF REQUIREMENT stage at which the service chiefs have to say 'Here's what we definitely want'.

The word 'definitely' is perhaps an overstatement since the services may have to alter their requirement during the lengthy processes that follow. Such alterations are generally referred to as *moving the goalposts,* an act which often prompts displays of crocodile tears by the contractors concerned who may put on a fine show of indignation whilst their accountants and contract lawyers pore over their desktop terminals working out just how much extra money they can wring from the changed circumstances.

Sometimes the ministry may leapfrog the PROJECT DEFINITION stage and go straight into what is known as FULL DEVELOPMENT. This may come about either because a particular piece of equipment is needed in a hurry or because the ministry considers that it has already done sufficient preparatory work on other related projects. Omitting Project Definition can be a neat way of cutting the length of the procurement process. Thus 'Bridging for the Nineties' which as we have seen grew out of 'Bridging for the Eighties' not unreasonably, went straight into Full Development on the evidence of earlier work. However, such instances apart, omitting Project Definition can lead to some spectacular foul-ups. The general rule for the layman who wants to know the reason why a project has got out of control is

> *first ask whether the ministry has been playing leapfrog.*

All being well the award of a production contract follows the completion of a series of trials at the end of the Full Development phase. Quite apart from the fact that these trials can go wrong the procedure is nowhere near as straightforward as might be implied by that simple statement. Despite all its power the Equipment Policy Committee does not control the money. That is the responsibility of an OFFICE OF MANAGEMENT AND BUDGET which administers the so-called LONG TERM COSTINGS, and it is the way that a project is likely to impact on its ten-year estimate which determines the pace of new equipment programmes. Moreover a FINANCIAL PLANNING AND MANAGEMENT GROUP sits somewhere between the OMB and EPC balancing the budget and has the final say on whether there is sufficient money available for each project.

Add any local difficulties which the MINISTRY OF DEFENCE might have in wringing money from THE TREASURY and the by no means uncommon situation of the selected contractor failing to deliver on time and it is not difficult to see why large programmes take so long to come to fruition. Typically a major system can involve the contractors in around eleven years' work before the equipment concerned enters service. However that is just the

THE THREAT

◄ IDENTIFYING
THE THREAT

◄ WHAT WILL IT BE
IN N YEARS' TIME?

◄ INTELLIGENCE STAFF
IDENTIFIES AND
INFORMS THE SYSTEM

THE SYSTEM

▶ THE SERVICE CHIEFS AND THE MINISTRY SCIENTISTS SET THE STAFF TARGET

▶ EQUIPMENT POLICY COMMITTEE ORDERS A FEASIBILITY STUDY: WILL IT WORK?

▶ SERVICE CHIEFS AND THEIR ADVISERS FORMULATE A STAFF REQUIREMENT

▶ PROCUREMENT EXECUTIVE AWARDS A CONTRACT FOR PROJECT DEFINITION

▶ Whilst they are doing this THE SYSTEM is asked to find money for the next stage – FULL DEVELOPMENT

▶ TRIALS: WILL IT WORK?

YES. Go to a Full Production Contract

NO. Start preparing excuses and hope that you get it right before THE THREAT begins to pull ahead contractors' work. By that time the project will also have taken up around three-and-a-half years of 'bureaucratic time' most of which will have to be completed between the various stages. With only one year overlapping, the total gestation time can be as much as thirteen-and-a-half years.

The Ministers

So much for Whitehall – although of course we shall hear much more of the problems that **The System** creates for itself. What about the ministers? Is their word law?

The MINISTER OF DEFENCE and his MINISTER OF STATE FOR DEFENCE PROCUREMENT have a hand in the major projects and although it is a rather grey area it seems that full ministerial approval has to be sought for any procurement over £25 million. Although £25 million does not buy very much defence equipment, and indeed in the United States would be considered to be a very modest sum, this threshold means that a great deal of procurement takes place with at best little more than a formal notification to the ministers. It also means that there are many hotly contested programmes away from ministerial gaze in which there is a temptation for the contractor with fewer scruples – or to use a more charitable description, a highly-developed instinct for gambling – to submit what the industry likes to call a *low ball bid* in which he may or may not have got his sums right.

Not surprisingly the ensuing contracts have been known to fail spectacularly, with one contractor having been said to be on course to lose around £6 million on a contract valued at slightly less than £18 million – not a matter to concern the ministry unduly since it was a fixed-price contract in which the luckless supplier has to foot the bill for his mistakes.

THE CABINET – through one or other of its many committees – will probably become involved in any major procurement over £25 million if it seems that it will become politically sensitive. Very rarely, when an issue has achieved a very high profile, it will be brought before the full cabinet, but usually the fate of the sensitive procurement will be determined by the OVERSEAS AND DEFENCE COMMITTEE which has the Prime Minister of the day at its head, or by a specially-convened *ad hoc* committee which could also be chaired by the PM.

■

The Sexy Issue

Not unnaturally **The System** views decisions by ministers to take a hand in particular procurement as events to be treated with great solemnity. However away from the Cabinet and its committees there are many other politicians with an axe to grind on matters of defence or who may see themselves as experts on a particular aspect of the subject. **The System** views their parliamentary questions and other attempts to gatecrash the parties it holds in its secret gardens as a darned nuisance.

Whenever they ask the price of a Tornado aircraft or a battle tank, they'll be told

'It is not our policy to disclose information of this nature'.

If they ask how much the ministry has paid to a particular contractor in the year just ended they are likely to be told that

'the information cannot be provided without incurring disproportionate cost'.

When, as on one occasion, they ask what was the disproportionate cost of providing such an answer they are told that

'a figure could not be provided because of the disproportionate cost of establishing it'

and the entire process seems to be in danger of sinking to the level of knockabout farce.

Nevertheless industry hopefuls continue to queue up at the MPs' doors and buy them jolly good lunches at Lockets, the Royal Horseguards Hotel and other convenient Westminster dining rooms in the hope that they will rally behind their various causes. In practice the MP is really looking for what he likes to call a 'sexy' issue on which he can ascend to the dizzy heights of headlines in the quality daily newspapers. Aeroplanes are sexy provided that their wings sweep backwards and they can fly at speeds in excess of 1000 mph. Tanks are sexy. Warships are very sexy. It is something of a paradox that in an age dominated by computers and information technology the products of any business that conjurs up visions of men in flat caps and mufflers trudging to work through mean streets with lunchboxes under their arms are sexy. Mumbo-jumbo, talk of things that glow or buzz or which sound sinister is sexy.

Even then though the MP can make the most terrible mistakes. One hopeful seized on the fact that a Volumatic Disintegrator had been delivered to an army missile range. What manner of terrible machine was this, he asked the minister responsible for such matters, and what destruction would it heap on the Queen's enemies? None, he was told. Disintegrator is the trade name of a rather efficient paper-shredding machine manufactured by the Volumatic company.

Beware of the Watchdogs

In contrast, anything in black boxes, software, command and control systems and radar are rarely sexy enough for your average backbencher. Move him towards the front benches and he might make a few tentative advances, but by and large they have all the sex appeal of cold rice pudding. The only way to spice them up is by suggesting that an entire industry might founder if it does not get a particular order. This is the political equivalent of a dose of powdered rhinocerous horn which although it might make the politician squirm excitedly for a limited period, like most aphrodisiacs, is no guarantee of an enduring relationship.

The exceptions to this rule – although they too still seek the sexier subjects for their inquiries – are the two House of Commons committees, the DEFENCE COMMITTEE and the PUBLIC ACCOUNTS COMMITTEE. The PAC occupies a position in a triangular relationship between Parliament, the independent office of the Comptroller & Auditor General and the various government departments. The Ministry of Defence is required to tell the PAC of any programmme on which it anticipates spending more than £100 million but in its relationship with it often displays a fair cross section of the disingenuous devices which took the TV series *Yes Minister* to the top of the ratings. There have for example been well-founded suggestions that rather than report some rather sensitive programmes likely to cost more than £100 million to the committee it breaks them down into a number of smaller projects. Then there was the occasion when at a public hearing a member asked the CHIEF OF DEFENCE PROCUREMENT if he could provide the committee with a sight of a Memorandum of Understanding between HMG and a foreign government. Certainly it could be, provided the member was left in no doubt that the CDP would be very happy to produce the document – provided, of course that there was nothing in it which would make it inadvisable that the committee should see it.

One of the more memorable clashes between the PAC and the ministry occurred in the early 1960s when the committee became aware that an army depot held a stock of 1,250,000 pairs of boots – that is to say around five

pairs for each man who had taken the Queen's shilling. 'You should not have bought them', it told the ministry, which promptly went out and sold the lot for £576,000 – thereby incurring a loss in the region of one million pounds!

Like the PAC, the Defence Committee has a watchdog role. In particular it keeps an eye on major defence programmes which its instinct tells it have ingredients which could produce unwanted problems. The committee has the power to take public evidence from the senior civil servants responsible for these programmes. However since the Parlimentary Committee system can be traced back to the seventeenth century when the diarist Samuel Pepys sat in parliament and served as Secretary to the Admiralty, there has been ample time for Whitehall and Westminster to develop rituals for such meetings which in generally well-mannered elegance and complexity often rival the courtship of the ruff and reeve. Unfortunately like that oft-observed wildlife ritual the public session is conducted before an audience of knowing enthusiasts – all the young hopefuls and old soldiers from the offices headed by those sitting in the hot seat – and like avian courtship, often seems to outsiders to have a disappointingly brief finale.

The ministry has become highly proficient at avoiding the issues which are likely to cause it embarrassment. At a 1989 SELECT COMMITTEE hearing on the use of manpower by its PROCUREMENT EXECUTIVE – the branch of the MOD that has the responsibility for actually buying the equipment – the man from the ministry revealed that a management audit at the Royal Naval Armaments Depot at Beith in Scotland had disclosed a situation in which 'the task of the establishment had got out of line with current strength'.

This meant that no fewer than 400 of Beith's 2000 employees were surplus to its real needs.

To make matters worse he confirmed that there were several thousand staff elsewhere in the ministry who he considered to be 'fat in the organisation'. When the committee's chairman suggested that it was 'awful management' to retain such surpluses within individual empires until such time as the audit team arrived, the ministry's representative took issue with him and in the process exposed a fine point of management practice that could provide even logicians with food for thought. He replied:

'If you do not believe there is fat in an organisation as large as the Ministry of Defence there is really no justification for having a management audit team is there?'

Industry – 'Give us the Tools and we'll Finish the Job' – eventually

The United Kingdom's DEFENCE INDUSTRY is said to comprise around ten thousand individual businesses ranging in size from giants like GEC down to small precision engineering workshops employing less than twenty persons. It also includes a great many companies which are not generally perceived as being in the defence business but derive a considerable income from keeping the wheels of the defence machine lubricated – quite literally so in the case of Shell, BP and Esso.

Although this varied assortment of industrial talent is not as hemmed in by departmental considerations as the ministry, which takes the greater part of its output of defence-related products, it too has its own rituals. A cynical observer once likened the long-established British defence contractor to the old-fashioned publican. That worthy was wont to stand behind his bar resplendent in a check waistcoat, sporting a diamond studded tiepin, double whisky in hand, discussing with other members of his exclusive club – the local Licensed Victuallers Association – the special status which they enjoyed because it was the local police and Justices of the Peace who approved their licences to trade. The event most likely to bring this self-congratulatory exchange to a temporary halt was the arrival of the bookmaker's runner to collect their bets on the day's horse racing – this was of course in the days before the law permitted betting shops.

That comparison is probably no longer entirely valid. It is not simply that better value for money has appeared high on the list of priorities handed down by goverment. The boom in defence spending of the early 1980s – which led to many of the more spectacular cock-ups – led many outside what was generally described as the defence industry to seek a slice of the action. The peace of the cosy club was shattered by the arrival of tradespeople. Its members were suddenly under pressure from a customer who wanted a sharp reduction in the number of *cost-plus* contracts in favour of *fixed-price* deals in which the onus was on them to deliver on time and within agreed prices. To make matters worse THE CITY, a collective term used to describe the new generation of sharp young men, who to use their own terms *followed* the defence contractors, was looking for a better *bottom line*. In short the people who had put the money into defence were looking for a better and quicker return on their investments.

In such circumstances it is hardly surprising that industry should have developed its own rituals. For the most part these are designed to convey the impression that it is simultaneously producing a worthwhile *bottom line* whilst being given the hardest of times by a government which does not understand its problems. When the pressures on the companies increase their response is to turn on the government.

> 'They have no industrial strategy ... How are we to keep the City happy if they make us dig deep into our pockets to fund research and development? ... By opening up its contracts to competition the ministry is driving our profits down to the point at which we are in danger of looking unattractive to investors ... But don't quote me old boy I'd rather not run the risk of upsetting anybody.'

The trick is never to shatter the illusion that you are doing very well indeed with the work that you are doing for that ministry. Thus virtually the entire spread of its activities has become protected behind serried ranks of public relations men who have succeeded in elevating whitewashing to the status of an art form.

The INDUSTRY PR MAN is engaged to convey the impression of a business presided over by the brightest and best who manage to keep it on station on the frontiers of technology without making any of those errors of judgement which distinguish their competitors. Mistakes are things that other people make. However sometimes even these sophisticated front-office operators go spectacularly wrong.

When a tank manufacturer invested heavily in taking a trainload of City financial experts to see just how good it was at its job, its latest tank, the star of the show, failed to start and then failed to find its target.

When an anti-aircraft system manufacturer flew a planeload of journalists many miles to see its brainchild in action it repeatedly let the target fly past unscathed.

So generally the rule is 'talk about it as much as possible, only show it publicly when you can be sure that it'll work properly – and whatever you do don't suggest that it has ever failed'.

What They Really Mean

Hopefully by now the reader will realise that **The System** is much more than a way of regulating the £20 or so billion that the government is spending on the defence of the nation each year. Careers, companies, political reputations, and the Whitehall oddity known to insiders as *the established position* all have to be as vigorously defended as the airspace around potential battlefields – and by the use of tactics in which *stealth* is as important as it has become in those skies. Whilst the aircraft builders wrestle with the expensive *stealth* technologies which have driven the cost of each of the US Air Force's B-2 bombers to around the $500 million mark, the wordsmiths are fighting their own battles to ensure that B-2 and a host of other programmes win the battle for public money. To assist them in their endeavours a universal language has been devised to make sure that as few people as possible in the wide world outside really know what's going on. This brief selection of phrases may provide an insight into the way in which they are playing the game and a flavour of the way in which **The System** works.

Total success
In 1984 viewers of a US television programme watched a film about some of the shortcomings of the US Army's Sergeant York anti-aircraft gun which was being developed by Ford Aerospace under a $4.5 billion contract. There had been some concern about the way in which the contract had been awarded – the Army had apparently counted near-misses during trial firings as hits – and the

word was out that not only was the gun not performing at all well but also that its cost was rising on some components by nearly 2000 per cent. With $1.5 billion spent and no solution in sight the US authorities decided to call a halt to the programme. The film the US viewers saw showed Sergeant York repeatedly missing targets only 100 yards distant, and eventually hitting a helicopter drone target only when its altitude was reduced to below 300 feet. When the TV reporter asked the programme manager (a US Army general) for his opinion of this abject performance, the general replied that 'it was absolutely a total success'.

Sergeant York's makers, Ford Aerospace, were not much better, claiming that at a subsequent trial the wretched gun had destroyed six out of the seven aircraft targets and three out of three helicopters. What, according to some authoritative sources, they did not say was that the airplanes had to be flown in front of the gun in straight lines many times before the kills were scored and that four of the aircraft were apparently destroyed by the range safety officer after he became concerned that they might stray from the range and cause damage elsewhere.

So watch out for people using *total success*. It is only rarely used as there is a risk that it might sound altogether too glib, and the chances are that it will only be used when somebody is in deep trouble.

Gold plating

Gold plating is rather like picking your nose. It's something the other fellow might do and which you certainly would not want to be seen doing. Nevertheless quite a lot of people do it. *Gold plating* occurs whenever a potential user loads up his specification for a piece of equipment that he needs with features that are not absolutely necessary. It can be a form of ego trip but watch out for the manufacturer who says to the user 'did you know that you can have such-and-such a feature … of course it would cost you a bit more but ... .

Capability
This is a word that is often bandied about in defence circles and has a definition depending on who is using it. If you are a serviceman you may use it to describe something that your enemy already has and that you don't have. So when you talk about a gap in *capabilities* you are in effect saying 'The bad guys have it and I need the money so that we can have at least the same'. Alternatively if you are a politician or a ministry official who has been closely involved with a programme for an item of equipment that has reached service without attracting too much opprobrium then you may justifiably claim that it represents a significant increase in *capability*. If you are in industry, having *capability* is the equivalent of saying 'gissa job'. It's something you are pretty certain that your company possesses but which you must convince the ministry beyond any shadow of a doubt that it possesses.

In the hands of a skilful player *capability* can be used to great effect. Thus a government official or a minister under pressure because ships are about to go to sea without a command system and with certain of their weapons unable to distinguish between friend and foe, might speak almost dismissively of a *somewhat reduced capability* if he is trying to wriggle out of some of the blame for the deficiency.

Slippage
A rather modish euphemism that has replaced the too specific *overrun*. A failure will almost inevitably result in a project taking more time and costing more money. *Time and cost overruns* are precisely what occur, but once such harsh language is used about a project, it could be damned for all time. Better by far for all concerned that *slippage* is used to convey the impression of a more graceful descent into confusion, despite all of their best efforts. It is the

defence procurement man's equivalent of the cartoon housemaid's legendary apology 'it come apart in me 'ands mum' as she surveys the broken chinaware.

Undergoing extensive trialling
'We are fearful that it'll break.'
Slippage usually follows.

Extended trialling
'It broke.'
Now we are into *slippage*.

We have no knowledge of any such incident
A phrase used by spokesmen when faced with irrefutable evidence that a piece of defence equipment has failed.

Move to the right
Under no circumstances should a *move to the right* be confused with *slippage* – although unhappily newcomers often fail to make the distinction. In theory when governments *move things to the right*, ie further into the future, they do so as the outcome of careful and mature consideration of the various factors which are likely to impact on both the nation's economy and its defences. In theory too nobody moves anything to the right when they can possibly avoid doing so. In practice they are doing it all the time because there is never enough money to do all that they want to. Since *moving to the right* is probably the biggest single cause of equipment being out of date by the time that it enters service nobody ever admits to being the person who took the decision – and for all we know, it could be that **The System** can do it without putting the Black Spot on individuals' careers.

Contractual negotiations are in progress
Now we have a sporting chance of being able to *move it to the right*.

Get better money
Payments over and above the original contract award in order to enable contractors to remedy serious – and expensive – problems which neither they nor the ministry had foreseen. Since in theory there is no way in which *get better money* can be paid on a fixed-price contract extracting it from **The System** provides industry with one of life's great challenges.

Political decision
A decision to purchase a piece of defence equipment which flies in the face of commercial reason is called a *political decision* by everybody except politicians who prefer to call it common sense. The important thing to note is that a successful contractor will never admit to benefitting from a *political decision*. A sure sign of a *political decision* is the contractor's use of the statement

> *'You have my word for it that we won fairly and squarely on price and technical merit'.*

Commercial in confidence
'We're not going to tell you how much we paid for it.' Often used when the Ministry of Defence wants to conceal the price it paid for something so that the manufacturer can put a hefty mark-up on the price he charges his export customers.

An unnamed Middle Eastern customer
Usually Saudi Arabia. Less frequently Jordan.

It is not our practice to comment on such matters
Used in reply to written Parliamentary Questions – often where there are suggestions that Saudi Arabia, *special weapons* or *classified projects* might be involved.

Special weapons
Nuclear shells, bombs, warheads, and depth charges.

Classified projects
Something we must not be told about. A category which includes Trident, some other types of nuclear weapon and secret communications projects which, like Zircon and Pindar, have often been openly discussed in not only the trade press but also in the quality daily newspapers.

3

FLIGHTS OF FANCY

No matter what they might say publicly, deep down in their hearts, governments don't like airmen very much. Airmen are expensive.

When one of the leading *think tanks* in the United States was asked to find out the dominant characteristics of the three services it reported that the Navy usually got what it wanted and the Army usually did what it was told to do without complaint. The Air Force's view of life tended towards the happy-go-lucky 'put wings on it and we'll fly it'.

Putting wings on things costs money. The think tank might also have found that the airman is happiest when he is flying fast – a process that digs deep into government money. Anybody who grew up during World War II will tell you that it was the people with the stubby biplanes with open cockpits and bulbous radial engines who got beaten. The winners were the people with the sleek monoplanes.

Because the ambitious airman doesn't want to be seen flying around in last year's model, governments have often had to spend heavily to keep pace with his requirements. Their job has been made all the more difficult by the fact that only eighty-six years separate the

Wright brothers' first flight from the latest MIGs, Mirages, Tornados and $500 million B-2 Stealth bombers. So much has happened in a relatively short time that it is hardly surprising that those who have the task of satisfying the airman's urge to head off into the wide blue yonder in ever-more elegant machines should often find themselves over-taken by the course of events.

■

Too Many Cuckoos

Inevitably there have been monumental miscalculations. The first came with the end of the 1914–18 war. The people who from time to time recall the triumphs and tribulations of Britain's aircraft industry never mention the aptly named Sopwith Cuckoo, a land-based torpedo bomber which began to roll out of the hangars in June 1918. Perhaps that is because the very mention of the biplane ought to trouble both ministerial and industrial consciences. Too late to take a useful part in the 1914–18 war, the Cuckoo equipped only one peacetime squadron for a period of just over three years before it was withdrawn from service. Yet the luckless government of the day had to pick up the bill for a total production run of no less than 132 Cuckoos, most of which had spent the greater part of their lives earth-bound.

The Cuckoo left the nest at a time when despite strict financial limitations on defence spending, aircraft had only short operational careers. In 1922 the Avro Aldershot was selected for the RAF because somebody believed in the idea of a single-engined heavy bomber. In the event the fifteen aircraft it acquired served in a single squadron for only two years, but at least when they were withdrawn there was general agreement that the single-engined heavy bomber did not have a future. In the years that followed the Air Ministry had the thankless task of trying to keep the British aircraft industry alive at a time when there was not enough money to go round and not a lot of political will to invest in warplanes.

The result was that the industry – and indeed the Royal Air Force – got used to the Air Ministry handing out its orders for airplanes in penny packets. For their part the planemakers seemed content to survive on handouts from Whitehall, made little serious effort to open up civil markets and more often than not sat back and waited whilst the government did most of the research work for them – at the customary bureaucratic pace. Admittedly brilliant exceptions like the Supermarine Spitfire, Hawker's Hurricane and the Rolls-Royce Merlin engine sprang from a creative period in the mid-1930s, but as the new industry that was needed to take them into mass production gathered momentum the Air Ministry continued to take delivery of fleets of lumbering biplanes. The last of these, the Gloster Gladiator, began to enter service in 1937 just under a year before the Air Ministry was to issue the specification which begat the Typhoon, a monoplane which it envisaged – far too optimistically as it turned out – as a successor to the Spitfire, which itself had still to enter squadron service.

■

Why Botha?
Or, With Friends Like That
Who Needs Enemies?

It is not unreasonable to argue that had the RAF not got its hands on these biplanes then it would have had nothing at all on which to make itself ready for war. On the other hand by years of buying small batches of aircraft that were quickly overtaken by the course of events, the Air Ministry had unwittingly – **The System** always makes its mistakes unwittingly – started a series of blunders that has dogged its successors and the luckless British tax-payer right up until the present time.

There were, for example, the three twin-engined aircraft which the Air Ministry chose for RAF Coastal Command. All had been ordered for delivery in the early 1940s. One of the two land-based torpedo bombers, the Beaufort, was built by Bristol, a company which already built the twin-engined monoplane Blenheim bomber and clearly knew what it was doing. Not so Blackburn which had not built a land-based military airplane since 1918 as it had subsequently specialised in biplane flying boats and carrier-borne aircraft for the Navy. Popular legend has it that its Skua was a rather difficult aircraft to fly and was at its easiest to handle when it was in a dive, but that didn't deter the Air Ministry. In 1936 it ordered no fewer than 442 Blackburn Botha land-based twin-engined mono- planes without even waiting for a prototype to be built. In a further display of confidence the ministry eventually increased its order to 580 aircraft, the first of which flew its first operational mission in August 1940. If Botha had just been difficult to fly the pilots might have come to terms with it – after all aviators are known to like a challenge. But Botha was not just lethal to fly. Loading it with a torpedo so impaired its performance that it had no useful range. Twelve weeks later the RAF finally shook its head and said in effect that it already had enough problems with the Germans and could manage without the underpow- ered Botha and its nasty flying habits.

The Bothas were promptly relegated to operational training schools – presumably on the principle that once a pupil had done his stint in a Botha he would go more willingly into combat – but elsewhere the RAF was struggling with its twin-engined Saro Lerwick monoplane flying boats. Saro had built a number of good flying boats so it is not entirely clear why it got the Lerwick so disastrously wrong. The RAF already had a good four- engined flying boat, the long-range Sunderland, and from the appearance of the Lerwick it seems that the Air Ministry thought that a scaled-down version with a range of around 1500 miles would be a good idea as part of the package that included the Beaufort and the Botha. When the Lerwick entered service in December 1939 it promptly showed itself to be a particularly ugly customer, unstable to fly and with very nasty stall characteristics. It was soon grounded and by October 1940 had to be grounded for a second time before being finally withdrawn from service in April of the following year.

The last of the twenty-one Lerwicks was delivered to the RAF in the month following the decision to withdraw it from service.

Thus during the long months of 1940 when the nation's fortunes were at their lowest a significant part of the hard-pressed aircraft industry was doggedly churning out flying boats that couldn't fly very well and user-unfriendly torpedo bombers that lacked the range to deliver their torpedoes anywhere near the enemy.

■
Defiant to the End

Meanwhile there were problems with fighter aircraft. Probably the most disastrous was the Boulton Paul Defiant, a bold new concept embodying a turret power-operated behind the pilot carrying four Browning machine guns. Unfortunately this novel feature left Defiant particularly vulnerable to attacks from the front and beneath, and after heavy losses in this way in August 1940 the aircraft was re-assigned to the night fighter role. It continued to serve in this capacity until July 1942. It comes as little surprise to learn that production continued until February 1943 by which time nearly 1100 Defiants had passed into RAF hands. Admittedly some became target tugs and others were adapted for air-sea rescue but the entire episode was one of the most costly of the ministry's wartime miscalculations.

The twin-engined Westland Whirlwind served for only two years and in the process earned itself a reputation as a temperamental performer. Whirlwind's major problem was that it was no good at all at high altitude, but that did not deter the Air Ministry from asking its makers Westland to build another twin-engined machine, the Welkin, for high altitude work.

Eventually sixty-seven Welkins were built but never used operationally.

The Wrong Airplane
at the Wrong Time

Our old friend *slippage* was at least partially responsible for some of the ministry's problems. Then as now, industry was keen to claim that it was rarin' to go on its contracts. Yet although the ministry had been expecting Vickers to have delivered 96 Wellesley bombers by the Spring of 1937, it had received only twenty-two – which probably did not matter too much because they were already at least obsolescent. One of the aircraft which quickly replaced the Wellesley in Bomber Command was the Fairey Battle – sometimes cynically described as a 'plane fit for heroes' – and by 1937 the Battle programme had also fallen badly behind schedule with deliveries running at only around half the scheduled rate. It too was obsolescent by 1939 and subsequently became a rather expensive trainer.

So what did the Air Ministry learn from such failures? Very little it seems. The Whitley bomber, by no means a failure and very much a stalwart of the early raids on Germany, performed its last bombing mission at the end of April 1942. But it too never really recovered from a rotten start to full production with the result that the

RAF took delivery of its last Whitley Mark V bomber on June 6th of the following year.

In January 1941 the ministry ordered two-hundred-and-fifty Vickers Warwick twin-engined bombers notwithstanding the fact that its prototypes had flown so badly that they had to be re-engined with a more powerful engine that was already in desperately short supply.

Adjudged a 'spectacular' failure in the extent by which they eventually failed to meet the specification, more than four hundred Warwicks were nevertheless built and served principally as 'gold-plated' air-sea rescue aircraft often replacing aircraft which arguably could have been flown on in that role for some considerable time.

■
No Shortage of Good Ideas...

It was probably too much to expect that when the war eventually came to its end, the ministry would take a look at all that had gone wrong and decide to make a clean start. Flying had already entered the jet age and weaponry the atomic age, but at first the ministry's attempts to wring enough money – to say nothing of commitment – from the newly installed Labour government in an effort to keep pace with such developments fell on deaf ears, and it was not until the early 1950s that its re-equipment programmes got into their stride. Its people had avoided the Cuckoo situations which had plagued their forerunners at the end of the 1914–18 conflict but had enough propellor-driven Mosquitos, Hornets and the like to keep them in business until the new jets arrived. However in the years that lay ahead they faced some new difficulties.

Such was the pace of change that industry was queuing up with good ideas, flying wings, giant flying boats, a jet propelled seaplane fighter, gigantic transports and lethal looking combinations of jet and rocket propulsion.

The choices seemed limitless but the cost was often staggering. The problem that the ministry could never really shake off was that from the mid-1950s onwards Britain was moving its troops back towards its own shores and did not need so much equipment. Buying 'just a few' pieces of defence equipment can be expensive and the ministry had a long history of placing contracts in such a way as to ensure that each of the planemakers got a slice of its business. The argument was 'that's the way we keep the industry healthy'. The truth was that it was a good way of keeping its hand in the tax-payer's pocket.

■

...and Plenty of Strange Decisions

Inevitably there were some nonsensical programmes. In the early 1950s the RAF acquired eleven only, specially designed, Avro Athena two-seat trainers, conforming to precisely the same specification as the Boulton Paul Baliol trainer – of which it ordered 162.

However the Athena was only a humble trainer and it was not until the ministry began to try much the same trick with jet fighters that it began to get into what would now be called 'serious money'. In October 1950 it ordered the first of its Hawker Hunter fighters for delivery in 1954. Nowadays it would tell the planemaker 'You get it to fly – or else!' In the 1950s the ministry was not going to upset the cosy relationships it enjoyed with its good friends in industry. The obvious thing to do was to order a second type of fighter interceptor just in case Hunter did not work. What more obvious solution than to order two prototypes and one hundred production aircraft from Supermarine, the company that had produced the Spitfire? Soon the bandwagon was really rolling, **The System** took charge and it ceased to matter whether or not Hunter might have been on course to become one of the RAF's most successful aircraft.

The Supermarine plane – now known as Swift – had begun its life as a research airplane rather than as a fighter but it certainly looked good enough to convince some of the ministry's experts that it was going to be a better proposition than Hunter, and with the Korean War having convinced the Labour government that it needed jet fighters quickly fifty more were ordered despite the fact that the prototype had yet to fly. When Swift got airborne it certainly flew fast, breaking the London to Paris record and the world's air speed record in rapid succession, but when the first twenty arrived at the squadrons it proved to be a dreadful fighter, not the least of its problems being the fact that it could not fire its guns at altitude without putting itself in harm's way. So it was that production of the Mark F1 was halted after only twenty aircraft, and the Mark F2 version after only sixteen – all of which were hurriedly passed to training establishments for ground instructional purposes. Twenty-five F3s were built but never reached operational units. There was some consolation for the ministry when it was found that later marks made an excellent photographic reconnaissance aircraft and served on in that role for about four years before being replaced by a reconnaissance version of the Hunter.

The total cost of the cancellation of the interceptor version was in the region of £22 million.

■
Up, Up and Away

By the time that Swift had settled down to its less spectacular role the airmen had a new toy. The Gloster Javelin was a very sexy airplane, a twin-jet delta-winged interceptor which carried sufficient electronic equipment to enable it to seek out its targets by day or night in all weathers. The Air Ministry had realised that with so much gadgetry aboard Javelin would be an expensive airplane, but its hopes that it would win export customers were dashed when the best prospect, West Germany, decided that a rather less sexy Fiat was the airplane that best suited its pocket. Javelin was a good airplane, which served on with the RAF until the late 1960s, but it differed from its predecessors in one important respect and took the ministry into some very unfamiliar and unfriendly territory.

Javelin was designed to carry four de Havilland Firestreak missiles with infra-red seekers which were locked on to the heat signature emitted by the target before they were launched against it. The ministry soon learned that the technology to develop such weapons – rapidly becoming *de rigeur* for the well-equipped aviator – could be very costly. In the process it made a series of spectacular miscalculations.

■

Think of a Number –
How the Rockets Hit the Pocket

Firestreak on its own would have been bad enough. When it started life in 1951 under the code name Blue Jay the ministry believed that the programme would cost around £4 million – by no means a modest sum by the standards of the day. By the early 1960s it had soaked up £33 million and its developers were asking for another £20 million to develop a Mark IV version. However Firestreak was not the only programme that was running away with public money, and the defence ministries – for this was before the three ministries were merged into a single Ministry of Defence – found themselves in what was to say the least a perplexing situation.

All three services wanted the latest technology. The Royal Air Force had asked for another relatively modest £12.5 million for the Blue Steel nuclear-tipped cruise missile to be carried by its V-bomber force.

By the time that it became operational in 1963, Blue Steel had knocked a £150 million hole in the public purse.

Then the airmen asked for another new toy, this time a ground-to-air missile to defend against enemy aircraft. They got the very impressive Bristol-Ferranti (later BAC and BAe) Bloodhound and although public confidence in the programme was dented when in later years Ferranti had to repay money it was found to have overcharged for parts of its work, the updated Mark 2 found customers abroad and still serves with the RAF after a quarter of a century.

Unfortunately at about the same time the Army also wanted £2.5 million for an air defence missile for a similar – but admittedly not identical – task. The soldiers, in the traditional manner of artillerymen, refused to compromise on what they saw as their responsibility and went ahead with the Thunderbird missile. Unfortunately they too had got their sums wrong.

The tax-payer was eventually presented with a bill not for £2.5 million, but for £40 million.

The Admiralty certainly was not going to be left out of the high-spending high-technology act. It wanted to acquire a missile called Seaslug to protect its warships and by pitching its estimate at only £1–1.5 million it excited little criticism.

That came later in the 1960s when the sailors were found to have spent £60 million on Seaslug and a further £70 million on the radar to acquire targets for it.

One observer was prompted to remark that 'the Admiralty rarely sees a need to excuse itself but when it does so it excuses itself over everybody else's boots'.

The redeeming feature of Seaslug and its costly contemporaries was that when the bills were paid at least the
services had some hardware. Other projects did not have
such a satisfactory outcome. The Army's plans to acquire
the Blue Water corps artillery missile ran through £32
million in just under five years – a notable piece of proflig-
acy by 1960 standards – before the accountants called a
halt to the project and the soldiers purchased an American
missile instead.

However it was usually the airplanes which hit the
headlines when they were cancelled. In 1952 when the
government of the day scrapped plans to build the giant
Brabazon airliner, hands were raised in horror at the
'waste' of nearly three-quarters of a million pounds on the
work that had been done. But prices were rising. Two years
later it was the turn of the Princess flying boat to be axed
– and the revelation that the project had already cost £9.1
million. The Vickers transport which fell by the wayside
in 1955 – without leaving the ground – set the taxpayer
back another £5 million, but by 1962 the costs of developing
new aircraft had risen to such an extent that cancellation
of the Rotodyne helicopter meant a write-off of around £12
million.

■

The Seamew Fiasco

No list of flying foul-ups would be complete without mention of the unfortunate Seamew. The Royal Navy's Fleet
Air Arm planned to acquire an aircraft which was in effect
a scaled-down version of its bigger carrier-borne aircraft.
Aircraft like Skyraider, Wyvern and Gannet were very
bulky and heavy. Seamew was conceived as an ideal
aircraft for reserve pilots and others who – not to put too
fine a point on it – did not fly as regularly as the young
men who heaved Gannets and the like around the skies.
What the Fleet Air Arm got for its money is said to have

been one of the most vicious unflyable little airplanes never to leave the hangar – so vicious in fact that it washed its hands of the project and twelve of the nineteen aircraft that were built were dismantled as they left the assembly line.

Seamew and all the other abandoned projects were consigned to a costly scrap heap that was eventually to include the very expensive TSR2 aircraft before Whitehall began to realise that it simply had to stop underpinning an industry that was unlikely to offer it the economies of scale – a trendy phrase that was beginning to be heard in the mid-1960s – that came with equipment developed for the US armed forces. As we shall see that was by no means the end of Whitehall's problems – the era of serious money had only just begun.

■

A Hit and Miss Business

The dawn of the missile era found defence ministries grappling with a new set of problems, many of which are at best still only partially solved. It was typical of the way in which most of the early weapons left something to be desired that one of the earliest of the US Army's hand-held heat-seeking ground launched anti-aircraft missiles locked itself onto the exhaust signature of the attacking aircraft. When it eventually caught up with the aircraft it did its job well, but the unfortunate infantrymen to whom it had been issued were quick to complain that by that time the attacker would have already flown over their positions and in all probability completely spoiled their day.

Predictably, the defence community was bedazzled by all the gee-whizz technology. But a lot of it did not work very well. In the skies above Vietnam the Americans' latest radar-guided air-to-air missiles flopped dismally. By far the most serious of their problems was that the pilot could only fire them after he had switched on his own radar. However by switching on he ran the risk of disclosing his position to his enemy and giving him a chance to get in with the first shot. Nearly as bad was the tendency of such missiles to become confused when confronted with two targets. More often than not they would hit neither and with that same infuriating logic that is all too familiar to inexpert computer users, steer a course between the two. Not surprisingly the bad guys soon learned to fly in pairs and the missiles' *kill-rate* dropped to an unacceptably low eight per cent.

The first of the American stand-off missiles were if anything an even worse waste of money than the radar-controlled weapons. In theory they ought to have enabled pilots to destroy ground targets in relative safety by launching their missiles whilst they were still outside the range of the ground defences. In the 1960s USAF spent nearly half a billion dollars on one such television-guided missile named Maverick destined for use in any future war in Europe. One of the more distressing of Mavericks's shortcomings was its complete inability to find its target in fog or even heavy rain.

Maverick had other failings, and even its improved version with an infra-red seeker has never really overcome criticism that the system is just not smart enough to permit the pilot to distinguish between genuine targets and any other hot objects that might be lying around on the battlefield. There was a subsequent example of the bedazzling and wasteful nature of missile technology when much later, in the mid-1980s, Mavericks were used in the Gulf War as a high-tech sledgehammer to attack low tech walnuts in the form of unarmed shipping, but in the meantime the Americans had been getting themselves into a similar set of problems with a laser-guided artillery shell called Copperhead.

Copperhead is steered towards a target selected by an observer equipped with a laser designator. The observer – often uncomfortably close to the action – keeps his laser trained on the target whilst the shell which is fired from a conventional howitzer many miles to the rear rides down its beam to make the kill. Except – yes, you have probably guessed correctly – when it is foggy or raining or when the battlefield is wreathed in smoke. This makes the laser-designated Copperhead of only doubtful use on a European battlefield – or indeed any battlefield where the target can get lost in smoke! 'The trouble with these guys,' said one American expert on the ways of the Army, 'is that they test their weapons on ranges in places like New Mexico where they've got plenty of space. You don't get a lot of heavy rain or fog in New Mexico.'

■
The Seventy-Six Bucks Damp Squib

Before returning to our main theme of the Made in Britain cock-up it is worth looking at a couple more US-made classics which illustrate the dangerous tendency for real life to become confused with gold plating. In 1976 the US Army decided that it wanted an anti-tank weapon not unlike the LAW80 described in Chapter 1. The US weapon was to be 'cheap and cheerful' and there was an initial forecast that it could be produced for $76. Yes that's right – as they have been known to say in the US 'watch my lips' – seventy-six dollars!

A price tag like that ought to have rung the warning bells and sure enough the contractors soon got to work *gold plating* the specification and in the process ensuring that they picked up a larger slice of added value. By 1982, with a little help from the Pentagon the price had increased tenfold but like LAW80 the missile's usefulness was in doubt. However the Americans do not have a *Right or Wrong Stand Still* rule, preferring instead to *re-evaluate the mission*. In plain English that means *'we have lost sight of our objective so let's double our efforts'*

and sure enough the Pentagon and its contractors were able to come up with a neat solution. They would tell the soldiers that they could only use the new missile against older tanks or against the side or rear portion of newer machines. That did not please the ordinary soldiers very much as in any event it only had a range of around 250 yards and they began to see a re-run of the problems that had bedevilled the early heat-seeking air defence missiles. When an influential senator complained 'you want something that hurts the enemy, not just pisses him off' and the accountants calculated that each of the 650,000 missiles on order was going to cost $1200 – nearly sixteen times the original estimate – the writing was on the wall and the army subsequently – but by no means in good grace – cancelled the project.

The Aquila programme provides another example of *gold plating* in action. After it had seen Israel's armed forces make good use of Remotely Piloted Vehicles, the US Army decided that it was time to get in on the act. The Israeli RPVs were not far removed from the familiar remotely-controlled model airplane but fitted with a relatively in-expensive video camera and the associated transmission equipment needed to get a picture back to the ground-based controller. However, this was not good enough for the Americans, who already had their own army RPV Aquila under development. Aquila had been conceived in the early 70s when, not to put too fine a point on it, defence was not a popular topic in the US. With the army having to fight for every dollar, its RPV, at first necessarily, carried an 'affordable' $100,000 price tag. However the enthusi-asm for RPVs peaked during the boom defence spending early-1980s and Aquila, which had never been a very good flying machine, suddenly found itself the focus of atten-tion from everybody who wanted to get reconnaissance and target designation equipment into the air. The problem was that since it had been designed with a low cross-section fuselage it became increasingly difficult for it to accommodate such ambitious payloads. The sky was the limit in every sense of the word and certainly not an element in which Aquila was ever at its ease. By the mid-eighties Aquila was carrying a $1 million price tag but still kept crashing with depressing regularity.

Astonishingly the disastrous programme was allowed to consume nearly $1 billion before it was decided to scrap it and seek a simpler solution.

4

THE IMPOSSIBLE TAKES A LITTLE LONGER (AND COSTS A GREAT DEAL MORE)

The Scots comedian Billy Connolly has a routine in which he imagines a nuclear weapons salesman demonstrating his wares to the Prime Minister. 'A real cracker...a wee smasher' he tells his potential customer – but the point that he is trying to make is that it's not a thing that you can 'take out on to the car park to try out' and in fact it could be filled with almost anything.

■

ALARMs and Diversions

British Aerospace must have had much the same thought in 1982 when it was trying to get the MOD to buy its ALARM missile. ALARM is an acronym for Air Launched Anti-Radiation Missile, a weapon designed to home in on the radar equipment seeking out the aircraft from which it is fired. A similar missile called HARM had already been developed in the United States. British Aerospace, which had yet to build ALARM and had nothing to show its customer, decided that the best way to sell it was to play on the weaknesses of its competitor. Since there is never any shortage of experts willing to find fault with a new weapon, British Aerospace decided to send one of its brightest young executives across the Atlantic to find people prepared to dish the dirt on HARM.

He did such a good job that the service chiefs eventually decided to recommend the Cabinet to award British Aerospace a contract – but only after the most senior of their number had looked hard – as only senior service officers can – at the young executive and declared 'Young man if I were you I would go out and find the largest possible piece of wood and keep on touching it until ALARM flies well.'

Of course it didn't, but long before designers realised that it certainly wasn't going to be right first time, the 'young man' had taken a step up the career ladder to a new employer leaving behind him one of the sorriest of recent defence muddles.

It had fallen to an organisation called the Rocket Motor Executive to decide whether to ask the government-owned Royal Ordnance Factories to make ALARM's motor as a subcontractor to British Aerospace or whether to ask the West German company Bayern Chemie to do so. It was only when the Royal Ordnance motor failed and the project began to fall far behind schedule that Whitehall began to realise that it had made the wrong choice and asked Bayern Chemie to let it have a design that would work. Ten years were likely to elapse between the recognition of the need for an ALARM-type missile and the RAF receiving the first production items.

Meanwhile HARM rockets were rolling off the Texas Instruments production line at a rate of around 150 per month. If Whitehall was to salvage anything from the mess it might perhaps have reclaimed part of that which it had spent on the wasted work on the Royal Ordnance motor. The solution seemed simple. Make a claim against British Aerospace. However the crafty contractor was more than equal to what, in the era of the cosy club, would have been seen as a mean and uncharitable threat. The planemaker replied

> *'And we will make a claim against the people who could not make the motor work who coincidentally are your Royal Ordnance rocket experts.'*

The matter might have stopped there had the government not been trying to sell the entire Royal Ordnance business. Since Royal Ordnance was claiming that it had incurred substantial extra costs in trying to get ALARM to fly, and the government for its part wanted to sell the company in good order, it agreed to pay it £19 million and for a time at least, to meet any claims that might be made against it by third parties who had been let down by its failure to make the motor fly.

By then it was 1987 and British Aerospace was locked in some tough negotiation with Whitehall on the terms which would be imposed on its further work on ALARM. The longer they argued, the longer the delay in getting ALARM airborne, and eventually the ministry was left with no option but to allow it to continue to develop the missile – albeit with its German motor – with the proviso that it would drop any claim that it might have had against

British Aerospace but agreed to reimburse RO to the tune of something in excess of the £19 million originally mentioned.

That being decided, British Aerospace – which at one stage considered that it was out of pocket to the tune of more than £100 million on the ALARM contract – offered to take Royal Ordnance off the government's hands, lock stock and barrel, for £190 million. The offer was subsequently accepted with the ministry agreeing in the process to purchase a significant proportion of its requirements of explosives and ammunition from British Aerospace for a period of several years ahead.

■

Nellie the White Elephant

Buying a pig in a poke – for that is what any untested system really amounts to – can lead the ministry into some very odd situations. So why does it do it? There can be many reasons, but one of the most compelling is a command from on high.

Histories of World War II bear countless examples of the way in which memoranda from Prime Minister Winston Churchill set lesser mortals off hotfoot in pursuit of all manner of technological moonbeams. To be fair some proved to be feasible and provided the inspiration for some quite remarkable technical achievements. On the debit side though, there were others which led to a wastage of scarce resources. Some, like the notion of an enormous man-made iceberg (to be known as Habakuk) which could serve as an aircraft carrier in northern waters, never really got on to the drawing board. One of the earliest, which made it to the trials stage and in the process consumed a great deal of bureaucratic and technical time was 'Nellie', a product of the early months of the war when the great man was still at the Admiralty. Nellie got its name from the Naval Land Equipment (NLE) Branch, which had taken a leading role in the development of the tank during World War I and nearly a quarter of a century later provided the senior service with an excuse to meddle in matters which were no longer its business.

Such land action as there was in the early months of the war was confined to France. From his seat at the Admiralty, Churchill conceived a way of ending the impasse between the entrenched Allies and their German counterparts that was already being referred to as The Phoney War. A fleet of giant tracked diggers would be despatched under cover of darkness to excavate deep trenches across the No Man's Land separating the two sides. Come the dawn, the British infantry and supporting equipment would surge through the newly-constructed earthworks emerging unscathed directly in front of the enemy positions. With a single leap, Jack (or in this case Tommy) would be free of the bonds of static warfare and in amongst the enemy who had presumably either slept undisturbed by the unfamiliar noise of the approaching excavators or had failed to appreciate the fate that was about to befall them.

The astonishing thing about Nellie was that Churchill got his way. A world-famous excavator maker was given a contract to produce a machine and in due course, long after the fall of France, Nellie was demonstrated to its proud parent, digging its way through the grounds of a stately home in the East Midlands. However that was the extent of Nellie's career and the massive prototype machines were last sighted languishing in an engineer plant depot awaiting sale to a scrapyard. Nellie has never ceased to fascinate the many military history freaks who have vainly tried to track down her dismembered superstructure. They at least never ask why it was that there should have been so much effort spent on such an obviously lost cause.

■
Nimrod

ALARM is a good example of what happens when a lot of people fall into the old theatrical trap of believing that 'it will all be all right on the night'. But at least at the time that this book was going to press it seemed that their confidence – but not the tax-payer – would be repaid and that ALARM would eventually become an albeit expensive part of the nation's armoury.

No such luck with the Nimrod Airborne Early Warning aircraft which, like Nellie, continued to soak up scarce resources long after the battle was lost. Nimrod has the dubious distinction of having become synonymous with managerial ineptitude, to the extent that whenever there is a hint that the men from the ministry have another flop on their hands Opposition politicians for decades to come will be gleefully telling their friends that 'It's another Nimrod'.

That is rather unfair on the Nimrod, which has given many years of reliable service as the Royal Air Force's maritime reconnaissance aircraft and is likely to remain in service until beyond the turn of the century. If Nimrod itself has a limitation it is that because it grew out of Comet – one of the earliest narrow-bodied jet airliners – it has relatively little space in which to stow equipment.

The need for an Airborne Early Warning – or AEW as the experts call it – aircraft arose when the threat from Soviet aircraft and cruise missiles escalated sharply. Part of the answer lay in having an aircraft with sophisticated radar which could survey a wide area, provide warning of *multiple threats* and exercise operational control to permit advanced interceptors like the Tornado to close on the right targets at the right time. In 1971 the RAF had converted twelve of its ageing Shackleton aircraft to provide early warning of attack but it had very quickly become evident that a more advanced system was required.

The Americans had such a system. Known as AWACS it was based on a Boeing airframe which had already been selected as NATO's answer to a need for an aircraft to provide radar surveillance and control of friendly fighters over Central Europe. The logical course for Britain would have been to follow suit and buy AWACS for the protection of the airspace over the North Sea. Instead in 1977 it dropped out of the NATO programme and decided to develop its own aircraft.

Nimrod was to be the platform for a system which would be developed by GEC's Marconi-Elliot subsidiary. It would not have AWACS' ability to control the interceptors, but if all went well it would be ready for full operational service before 1984, and the cost, it seems, was not expected to exceed a relatively modest £300 million. Nor was it a bad deal for GEC which was given the then fashionable *cost-plus* contract which guaranteed it the *cost* of development *plus* an agreed percentage profit.

The man behind the decision was Fred (later Lord) Mulley, a much-liked Labour politician who apart from the Nimrod decision is perhaps rather unfairly best remembered as the Secretary of State for Defence who nodded off to sleep whilst seated alongside Her Majesty Queen Elizabeth II at a military demonstration arranged in celebration of her Silver Jubilee as monarch.

Of course the decision was not Fred Mulley's alone. The government of the day saw the decision as likely to *save jobs*. *Saving jobs*, like *creating jobs*, is often used by politicians to embellish their decisions. The trick is to convey the impression that they really do have the ability to put a figure on the benefits which will flow from their decisions. The fact that a government which had only recently nationalised the aircraft industry could hardly be seen to be shopping abroad was hardly mentioned.

The Nimrod AEW very soon ran into difficulties. Despite bulbous additions to the nose and tail sections of its fuselage it lacked not only the space to accommodate the very complex range of electronic equipment necessary for its mission but also that in which to fit sufficiently powerful cooling systems to maintain the cramped equipment spaces at a workable temperature. This technological 'Catch-22' situation became even more complicated when the Royal Air Force decided that it would like its Nimrods to be able to control fighter aircraft in much the same way as the AWACS. It is not clear whether this was a classic case of asking for 'just that little bit extra' in the belief that it would become possible in due course. Whatever the reason, the harsh reality was that Nimrod lacked the computer processing power to do the job.

With a *cost-plus* contract in its pocket the contractor was certainly not going to complain about the uphill nature of the task it had been given. The ministry followed the *Right or Wrong Stand Still* rule and began to throw *get better money* at Nimrod in an attempt to cure its ills. Since it had never publicly admitted how much it had intended to spend on the project, it had a head start over its critics but by 1984 as the news of Nimrod's ills leaked out it became clear that nearly £820 million had been lavished on it and more than half as much again might be required to effect a cure. By this time *slippage* to at least 1987 was on the cards. During the ensuing fourteen months it became clear that even this was an optimistic forecast which could be adrift by at least three years. A great deal more money would have to be spent before Nimrod AEW was ready for service. To make matters worse, the longer its entry into service was delayed the greater the danger that the Royal Air Force would ask for new features to help it keep pace with the evolving **Threat**. Since Nimrod's problems included performing at around 40 per cent of target efficiency, an inability to differentiate between cars using the A1 trunk road and genuine targets, and on its worse days confusing stationary objects like buildings with the real thing, it began to look increasingly like a lost cause.

In 1985 the ministry had begun to get tough with its contractors – or rather tougher than it had been – and decided that the time had come for Marconi to deliver. It gave Marconi six months to get the system working and another £50 million with which to do it. Early in 1986 it bit on the bullet and, recognising that Nimrod's chances of recovery were slight, asked other contractors to submit their proposals for alternatives. Nobody is prepared to discuss their individual bids in too much detail but it seems that GEC – its credibility pretty badly dented – was prepared to accept another £650 million to get eleven aircraft in service by 1991 whilst the US plane maker Boeing bid £860 million for the supply of six AWACS aircraft. The ministry – not surprisingly in all the circumstances – treated GEC's claims with some suspicion, decided that it would be unlikely to be able to deliver before the mid 1990s and opted for Boeing's E3A AWACS.

The cost to the British tax-payer was about £200 million more than the GEC proposal of which the government was so suspicious. On top of the £800 million or so already spent it meant that the cost of the project had soared to around £1.5 billion – five times that of the original 'convenient' solution.

■ Buy it Abroad!

Faced with a major problem the government had no alternative but to look overseas to find a system that actually worked. Not surprisingly British industry lets out howls of protest whenever this happens. 'We'll get it to work don't you worry,' it says. 'All that it needs is time and money.' That said it usually goes into a fit of deep depression complaining to the media that the government doesn't understand it in much the same way as the tired businessman is said to talk to the bar girl about his wife.

There are few hard and fast rules to guide Whitehall. Sometimes it has seemed to have sailed very close to the wind. In 1937, two-and-a-half years before the outbreak of World War II, Vickers found itself unable to deliver a light anti-aircraft gun which was obviously very badly needed. Whitehall ordered a hundred guns from the Swedish Bofors company and arranged to make more of them under licence in the UK. Then after the Munich crisis it decided that it needed more and placed orders on suppliers in Belgium, Poland and Hungary. When it needed height-finders for its anti-aircraft defences it ordered them from Austria – showing an almost childlike trust by placing the order for the last batch in June 1938, three months after the German Army had marched into that country.

That might seem like a massive error of judgement. Certainly it was no worse than a 1937 decision to order shell and bomb production machinery from Germany – a move which conjures up images of men from the ministry waiting politely until Prime Minister Neville Chamberlain had finished reading from the paper to which he and the German Führer had put their signatures at Munich before saying

> *'Yes, quite so Prime Minister, but did Herr Hitler mention when we could expect delivery of the bomb machines?'*

Quite clearly there was little chance that Britain could have developed its own bomb-making machinery as war loomed ever closer and the ministry had to go out and buy it wherever it could. Today, the Trident submarine-launched nuclear missile, and the Boeing AWACS provide examples of generally fairly effective purchases of *off-the-shelf* equipment at better prices and with better delivery dates than would have been possible if the ministry had been obliged to start from scratch. However in recent years there has been an increasing tendency for friendly countries to get together to produce equipment that meets a common requirement. The most elegant of these collaborative arrangements is probably the European Fighter Aircraft – an airplane which answers a need which would be very expensive for the individual nations to satisfy with aircraft of their own making. There has been a number of successful collaborative projects. Nevertheless a number, like the Anglo-German attempts to set up a programme for a 'collaborative' Main Battle Tank and an international self-propelled howitzer – SP70 – have foundered and defence procurement people are having to learn to live with a nasty new problem – *continental-style bureaucratic time.*

Of course the ministry ought to know all about the extravagances that time can lead to. Nevertheless international collaboration, the to-ing and fro-ing between countries, the appointment of lead contractors in each, and the delicate tapestry of committee work take it into unfamiliar territory. When the ministry embarks on a collaborative project it usually finds itself dealing with joint venture companies representing the interests of the lead contractors, and possibly even inter-governmental management agencies – and the bureaucratic time and costs go up and begin to eat into the savings which it thinks it is making.

■

The Slowest Gun
in the West

SP70, the tri-national howitzer, first emerged in 1971 as a ministry *requirement* for a replacement for the British Army's obsolescent Abbot self-propelled guns. Two years later development got under way in partnership with West Germany and Italy, but although various prototypes were produced the partners never really sorted out their differences on how SP70 should be built. At first they could not agree about the use of aluminium to build its hull. Then, there was disagreement about another of its features, a novel ammunition magazine holding thirty-two 155mm shells which fed the gun via a complicated microprocessor-controlled automatic loading system. Reloading the magazine could only be effected through a hatch in the side of the turret, but since this left the ammunition handlers standing outside the protection of the turret and thus exposed to enemy shot, shell and even worse, SP70 would have to have been driven away to a quiet spot away from the action every time it needed to replenish its supplies.

Unfortunately whilst the partners tried to unravel these problems the technology began to slip away from them and would-be users began asking for a longer gun barrel to enable the gun to hit targets more distant than they had in mind when work on SP70 had begun. Eventually in 1986, after they could find no more com-pelling argument for persevering with the project than the vast sums of money that they had spent over the past thirteen years developing a gun that looked set to be ob-solete before it entered service, the three nations decided to abandon the entire project. From the British point of view the sorry saga came to an end nearly three years later in June 1989 when the Ministry of Defence placed a £300 million contract with VSEL for one-hundred-and-seventy-nine AS90 howitzers – a gun which the company had begun to develop at its own expense only after the SP70 project collapsed. Delivery would commence in the early 1990s, just twenty years after the first costly steps had been taken to replace the Abbot guns.

So it was perhaps hardly surprising that TRIGAT, an anti-tank missile being developed by Britain, West Germany and France, stayed stuck at the Project Definition stage for no less than seven years. That might seem like time enough to resolve most of the problems. But in 1988 on the day after Britain finally committed itself to the project and looked set for full development, a ministry representative told the House of Commons Select Committee on Defence that the ministry was still *some way from knowing* whether its preferred helicopter to carry the long range version of TRIGAT was going to be suitable for the job. Could it carry the required number of eight missiles as well as a decent payload of fuel? The ministry man went on to the defensive describing it as a *potential problem* – which in plain language means

> *Watch this space – we're on course for another cock-up.*

5

ALL AT SEA

We have already seen how the Royal Navy and its Lords of the Admiralty got their sums wrong on the Seaslug missile. The sailors are of course justifiably proud of their place as the Senior Service and, quite separately from the *think tank* view of navies as the people who get what they want, tend to go through life instinctively projecting themselves on to a slightly higher plane than their contemporaries in armies and air forces.

Possibly it is because of this attitude – often mistakenly percieved by those outside the charmed circle as 'toffee-nosed' – that history does not record whether the builders of the first triremes made the oars too short or whether the earliest fireships could be turned round by a change in wind direction and blown back into the midst of the fleet that had sent them blazing on their way. Certainly naval libraries are rather cheering places to visit with shelves crammed with Navy Lists, in which one can assume that everybody knows or knew everybody else, and tales of convincing victories, or at the very least, of a bunch of jolly good chaps snatching a win from the jaws of defeat.

They also reveal the extent to which navies care

about their big ships. Glossy coffee-table picture books and encyclopedias of naval architecture alike bear witness to a preoccupation that might be as worrying to psychologists as it often is to the politicians and civil servants. Today's admirals tend to shrug off the bills in excess of £400 million for a nuclear powered missile-firing submarine. It is, they say in their more expansive moments, the price of deterrence and hence freedom for us all. After all, they add, these are today's capital ships. In so saying they exude a quiet satisfaction that their big ships now go covertly about their ways far from the gaze of us lesser mortals.

■

The Battleship that Nearly Wrecked a Pub – but that was All it Did

Appropriately, the first of the Royal Navy's new Trident nuclear missile submarines is to be named HMS *Vanguard*. The previous ship to bear the name, the 44,500-ton battleship HMS *Vanguard*, stands out in the memory as a classic example of how not to run a navy. Laid down at the height of the war, *Vanguard* was launched in 1944 and when eventually completed in 1946 had cost the taxpayer £9 million, only one-fiftieth of the price tag on its successor, but a large sum for the day and age, which might have been justified if only the admirals could have found it a job.

In 1947 *Vanguard* was used to carry King George VI and Queen Elizabeth on a State Visit to South Africa and upon its return went straight into dock for eighteen months for a major refit. When the work was completed the Korean war was in progress and there might possibly have been a role for *Vanguard*'s eight fifteen-inch guns in providing supporting bombardment for the land forces. In the event, it was used as a training ship for about two years at the end of which time it went for another six-month refit. In 1954 *Vanguard* was nominated as Flagship of the Home Fleet and finally seemed set to realise its full potential. Eighteen months later the flag was hauled down and the pride of the fleet went into mothballs until the mid-1960s, when it was sold to the breakers. In what might have been a final gesture of defiance, *Vanguard* ran aground as it left Portsmouth harbour for the last time – much to the alarm of the regulars at Old Portsmouth's Still and West public house who had not hitherto considered themselves to be particularly at risk of being run down. With its refits and guns – which had originally been made for two World War I battleships and having been paid for by an earlier generation of tax-payers were not included in the £9 million price tag –

Vanguard had cost the British tax-payer somewhere in the region of £23 million.

The *Vanguard* fiasco came at about the same time as the admirals faced similar problems with their traditional cruisers. Although they were smaller than the battleships, the cruisers showed all the signs of being too unwieldy for a future in which power was likely to be projected by aircraft carriers and surface battles fought by a new generation of nimble warships, crammed to the gunwales and beyond with missiles and supporting electronic equipment. The Admiralty and subsequently the Ministry of Defence (Navy) nevertheless perservered with the cruisers and indeed adapted some of them to a role as helicopter carriers to bridge the gap before the development of the lighter aircraft carriers that were considered more attuned to Britain's less extensive global commitments. In the meantime, **The System** prevailed and the tax-payer was left with another massive bill – in this case £15 million – for the cruiser HMS *Blake*.

Like *Vanguard*, HMS *Blake* had been laid down during the war years, but launched too late to play a role in the defeat of Japan. Thus it was clearly a matter to be dealt with under the *Right or Wrong Stand Still* rule and accordingly the big ship lay uncompleted for the next nine years. The government was now facing the prospect of a withdrawal from some of its traditional bases abroad. The admirals took a look at some of their redundant and unfinished warships and decided that the time had come to complete *Blake*. The work took seven years, during which time the *state of the art* moved on, the infamous Suez affair came and went, and the government worked its way through several alternative nuclear strategies. So it was hardly surprising that when its fitting-out was complete HMS *Blake* was already out of date and had to be sent back to the dockyard for another year's work. As the additional work neared completion, preparations for the great day when *Blake* would join the fleet gained momentum. An 800-strong ship's company has already been posted, but at the last moment the Admiralty decided that the cruiser should be placed in preservation and join its mothball fleet.

The bill to the tax-payer for a ship which had no proper role and would probably require still further work before it was any use to the navy had already reached £15 million.

By this time, the navy was fighting most of its battles in Whitehall, where its clever policy of selecting its staff officers from those who were one rung higher on the promotion ladder than their counterparts in either the army or the air force made it possible to patrol the corridors of power with admirals in much the same way as it had once patrolled the high sea with splendid battleships. Whether this display of power made a lot of difference to the ships and their equipment is open to argument. Certainly the bills continued to rise with the introduction of each new class of warship. Nevertheless, when the battles moved out of the corridors, the Falklands War revealed glaring deficiencies in the navy's equipment, not the least being a lack of Airborne Early Warning aircraft. The navy had paid off its last AEW Gannets in 1978, but believing that the ill-fated Nimrod would eventually be available to it in a war had done nothing to provide even a temporary replacement. The upshot was that whilst the battle fleet was on its way to the South Atlantic its officers were examining ways in which they could botch up the surviving Gannets. These veterans included the 'gate-guardian' standing outside a Scottish naval base, one which had passed into the hands of an American enthusiast, and a couple more which were drawing the crowds in museums. Spares could also have been removed from five more unflyable machines lying in various states of decrepitude at airfields in the UK, Germany and Gibraltar.

Fortunately, the need for AEW equipment was solved without the need to resurrect long-dead airframes, but once the euphoria of victory had dispersed, the aftermath of the war in the South Atlantic left the Ministry of Defence with some very persistent problems. One of these was the cost of its ships. In the 1970s the navy had not been at all keen to co-operate with its counterparts in the Netherlands in a joint programme. One of the sticking points had been Dutch insistence on a somewhat shorter ship than the Royal Navy had in mind – not unreasonably since they wanted it to be able to fit the docks on their side of the Channel. That was not a matter on which the Royal Navy was prepared to compromise and instead it got its Type 22 frigates which are not only Europe's largest frigates, but also, at nearly £200 million apiece, the most expensive too. Since few navies really want such hideously expensive warships – to say nothing of their size – the Type 22 has been a non-starter in world markets. The men from the ministry have spoken of the cost of keeping pace with **The Threat** but believe that they might have tamed this problem in their latest Type 23 frigate. It might be easier to believe them had they not still been making some dreadful mistakes elsewhere. When they wanted to buy an Aviation Training Ship (RFA *Argus*) they decided to convert a merchantman rather than build an entirely new vessel. Admittedly a few eyebrows were raised when the Northern Ireland shipbuilder Harland & Wolff was given a £28 million contract to do the job, but nowhere near as many as shot upwards when it became apparent that the joint endeavours of shipbuilder and civil servant had failed to recognise just how much work was involved. Eventually Harland's directors had to tell its shareholder that the job had cost between £45 and £50 million more than they had anticipated.

> *'Never mind though,'* it said, *'we will claim damages from the Ministry of Defence'.*

Predictably the ministry said,

> *'But you didn't let us have our ship on time so we want liquidated damages from you'.*

Connoisseurs of the cock-up will have noted the use of the singular 'shareholder' in the preceding paragraph. Who was this singular shareholder? You've guessed correctly. **It was of course Her Majesty's Government**.

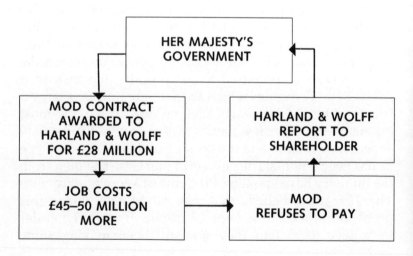

Out of Their Depth

The more sympathetic reader will of course argue that it was rotten luck or another demonstration of the universality of Murphy's Law – if a thing can possibly go wrong it will. That is as may be. The ministry has made less spectacular but none the less mind-bending mistakes. It is difficult to see how anybody could go wrong with as simple a vessel as an aluminium-hulled tender to service hydrophone arrays on submarines. The ministry did. The three such vessels it ordered in 1986 were found to be unable to attain their design speed, and in the very best seafaring traditions, it began the search for alternative roles. Seasoned observers foresaw the long series of lay-ups, refits and modifications which have usually characterised the more spectacular flops.

Strangely, the naval programmes which have run away with more money than any others in recent times have not produced flops. When in 1979 the Ministry of Defence decided that it would buy its future lightweight torpedo from the British manufacturer Marconi it knew that it was taking a considerable gamble. The modern torpedo is an underwater guided weapon with as much, if not more, complexity than those which are used on the surface. The Americans already had such a torpedo which could be modified to suit the ministry's needs at a cost of between £250 and £320 million but the navy wanted a superior weapon which it could be sure would penetrate the hull of every known submarine and those likely to emerge as **The Threat** in the years ahead. The servicemen eventually got the torpedo that they needed, but not until the cost of the programme had soared to more than £1.4 billion – for which price the navy could have had the American torpedo together with several new frigates.

The situation was, if anything, worse with the heavyweight torpedoes for launching from submarines. Those already available in the United States were capable of meeting British needs for a new anti-submarine torpedo which could defeat a new **Threat** in the form of the Soviet Alpha-class submarine. Moreover the ministry had not had a particularly easy time with its most recent heavy-weight torpedo, Tigerfish, which had eaten up £450 million – £22 million more than anticipated – from the time at which its development started in 1959 until its entry into service, seven years behind schedule, in 1974.

After a great deal of wrangling the Americans were eventually able to offer a price advantage of well over £100 million over Marconi's price for a home-made solution. However, if they thought that they were home and dry after such a competitive bid, they were to be proved sadly wrong. Marconi had the heat on the government at a time when jobs were a sexy issue, adding a neat bonus by assuring the government that an order for the torpedo which later became known as 'Spearfish' would help it bring down the price on Stingray. In the end the government made what industry calls a *political decision* and, although Spearfish had originally been estimated to be likely to cost only £155 million, let a contract to Marconi for £496 million. By the beginning of 1989 expenditure on Spearfish had risen to £594 million, the Naval Staff Requirement remained unfulfilled, and the ministry was preparing to open its requirement for Spearfish up to competition in an effort to secure *better value for money.*

■

Into the Expensive Unknown

Cost is only one of the navy's problems. Computer soft-ware, the brains behind the systems with which it controls its new generation of weapons, has given Whitehall a series of very unpleasant headaches. The cock-ups continue and to paraphrase the introduction of the old TV show *Dragnet*, 'only the language has been changed to protect the ministry'.

All manner of clichés have been used to excuse Whitehall's repeated failures. In the final analysis it seems that 'capability to respond to the evolving threat has been degraded as a consequence of a failure to provide sufficient front-end investment. Moreover the ministry has learned from experience of software-intensive projects and the type of problem that they can bring that they tend to be problem projects.' These phrases, culled from official statements, are Whitehall's equivalent of the football manager's 'at the end of the day the lads' heads went down and we are all as sick as parrots' after a six-nil thrashing. In short they mean that it is darned nearly impossible for **The System** to keep pace with all the changes that are happening on the software scene and, unless it puts the right sort of money into a project at the very beginning, its contractors won't be able to do so either.

The software problems are by no means confined to naval projects, but they have had the unfortunate consequence that the Royal Navy is likely to have to send perhaps as many as five of its latest frigates and two of their supporting auxiliaries to sea without automated command and control systems. It was not until after a couple of abortive attempts and the placing of the first contracts for the ships that the ministry and its contractors were able to get their acts together and come up with a system that was likely to be able to keep pace with **The Threat**. But it would take time to get into service. A junior minister cheerfully assured journalists that 'there are lots of things that the ship can do without its command system' but a senior naval officer had to confess to a parliamentary committee that the ship would have to be careful until it received its full system. Why? 'Well,' he explained, 'the link from the radar to the ship's defensive missile system does not *have* to pass through the command system – but if it doesn't the ship has no reliable way of differentiating between friendly and hostile aircraft.'

That might seem to limit the 'lots of things' to quiet trips round the lighthouse, but the ministry's man was able to reassure the committee that since the new frigate's job was primarily to hunt enemy submarines it would probably not be working too close to aircraft carriers anyhow. The other crumb of satisfaction which worried airmen might be able to derive from the situation, was the fact that in any event, development of the missile concerned (Vertical Launch Sea Wolf) had fallen behind schedule – and with a £400 million price tag has already cost the taxpayer at least £50 million more than the ministry had expected.

6

RIGHT FIRST TIME

In the summer of 1989 the House of Commons Public Accounts Committee published a report on an inquiry it had conducted into the reliability and maintainability of the equipment which the Ministry of Defence purchases on behalf of its customers the armed forces. One revelation which grabbed a minor headline at the time was that it costs the tax-payer around £1 billion each year for modifications and repair work to rectify the consequences of unreliability in the services' equipment.

The work found necessary as a result of the Jaguar aircraft failing to maintain the standards required by the ministry had already consumed around £496 million of public money and the expectation was that such spending would eventually account for around thirteen per cent of its entire whole life cost.

It was a report which caused more than a moment's panic amongst the defence industry's public relations men. The impression which they are at pains to convey is of an industry with an eye for detail that makes the average

Swiss watchmaker look as slapdash as the itinerant labourer who offers to tarmac your front driveway. Beneath the shiny surface, could it really be that these same paragons of virtue were actually skimping on *reliability and maintainability* in an effort to trim their prices to the most competitive level? Or is it that the ministry from whom they take their orders is unable properly to spell out its requirements?

Probably each is at fault in its own way. Certainly, when it comes to keeping its house in order, the ministry does not have a blameless record. When a young army officer was assuming responsibility for a part of one of the army's vehicle depots, he asked his predecessor

> *'What about those?' pointing to several neatly parked lines of elderly but obviously still unused large trucks. He was told: 'Whatever you do don't try to move them, their transmissions break and there are no spares in the country'.*

Came the day when there was no alternative but to move them and sure enough most of them broke down. Since the army had no use for the vehicles which were by that time obsolete this begs the question why it wanted to move them a distance of several thousand miles – but as we have seen that's the way **The System** works.

Industry too has also been far from blameless. In 1964 the ministry wanted to buy a bulldozer to fit on the army's Chieftain tanks and accordingly accepted a contractor's prototype subject to certain faults being remedied. Six years later – presumably the requirement had been *moved to the right* – it placed production contracts. When the first bulldozer set was delivered in 1972 the faults had been remedied, but it had an entirely new combination of mechanical, electrical and hydraulic faults. The obvious thing for the ministry to do was to call a halt to deliveries, but instead it allowed production to continue after having been told that most of the components had already been made for the remaining 97 kits that it had on order. It was yet another example of **The System** applying the *Right of Wrong Stand Still* rule and few followers of such situations will be surprised to learn that when the kits were delivered in 1973 they had yet another entirely fresh hydraulic fault. However that didn't matter too much because by that time the kits failed to align properly with the towing eye through which they should have been secured, and therefore didn't fit the tank anyhow. It was to be two years before the sets were finally *fit for purpose*.

The more cynical observers of industry affairs might not be surprised by such classics. There is no more pleasant windfall for a contractor than a nice fat contract to rectify problems bedevilling his equipment after it has been delivered to the ministry. By the same token contracts to supply spares can also keep him in clover long after delivery. It is at least a case of the more there are the merrier the supplier, until he eventually reaches the blissful moment when he can tell the ministry 'Well you know that the things you want are no longer in production ... but don't worry we can make them for you'. That is the juncture at which he throws his price lists away and thinks of a number. Whether the cynics are right in claiming that, whenever anything breaks, the contractor sheds a few crocodile tears whilst mumbling something like 'if only you'd given us a little more money at the time we might have prevented this unfortunate business – still never mind we'll make you a few spares' is open to speculation. However, in a cruel commercial world, it does not seem to be an unreasonable scenario.

With the exception of the army's tanks, vehicles ought not to present the ministry with too many problems. They are not high-tech, have none of the nasty frailties of electronic systems, and are rarely sexy enough to provoke a political storm. Yet since **The System** does not discriminate along such lines, the humble truck can easily become a drain on the public purse. Obviously the services need reliable trucks that can take a great deal of harsh treatment – so, quite reasonably, they always ask for a specification that in effect gives them a great deal of spare capacity. By common consent that is certainly not *goldplating*. Nevertheless, the more specialised the task, the greater the temptation to *goldplate* the specification. In one never-to-be-forgotten episode in its history the ministry (or War Office as it then was) decided that it needed an entirely new family of combat trucks and in so doing for a few years provided all concerned with quite literally a golden opportunity.

■
The Defeated Champ

One member of this family was the Rolls-Royce-engined Humber one-ton Combat Truck which despite having been found to be unsuitable for the purpose for which it was built is still to be found in service as the chassis of the armoured personnel carriers used by units in Northern Ireland.

Another, and by far the most notorious, was the Champ, an up-market successor to the ubiquitous wartime Jeep that was the outcome of the combination of the differing talents of the Austin Motor Company and Rolls Royce. The army never wanted the Champ. When they were told about it the more far-seeing soldiers said 'Thanks but no thanks'. It would be expensive to buy, complicated and difficult to maintain, would need a massive investment in spare parts, and above all would not be *soldier-proof*. That did not deter their masters who went ahead with a project which was to cost £16 million before, with the soldiers' worst fears found to have been fully justified, Whitehall called a halt, and in the process prompted some years of indecision over the best mix between *military specials* and *off-the-shelf* buys.

■
Off-the-shelf

The need for defence equipment to be *soldier-proof* was for a long time one of the major objections offered against *off-the-shelf* purchases of equipment that had originally been developed for civilian use. Since one of the earliest post-war cargo trucks purchased *off-the-shelf* for the Bristish Army regularly broke its front springs as soon as it was driven across even the gentlest unprepared surface, it is not difficult to see why soldiers should have become rather upset at suggestions that they should use the same types of lorry as their local haulage contractor. In more recent years use of the term has been extended to include purchases of equipment originally developed for use by the forces of another country – for example the Boeing AWACS – and that which like the AS90 howitzer has been developed as a private venture without government support.

Servicemen do not like buying *off-the-shelf* but have grudgingly accepted the need to do so as an inevitable part of the government's search for better value for money – something that not even they find easy to argue against, since better value for money, on the equipment side of the defence budget, leaves more on the manpower side to put in to their pay packets. In some parts of their inventory – the military truck is one – standards of quality and reliability have improved and they are less worried at the prospect of using the commercial item. Nevertheless two more examples from the world of wheels illustrate the extent of the gap between what the servicemen consider to be their needs and those of lesser mortals.

In 1988, when the Army made a great fuss about the number of engine failures suffered by its fleet of Land Rover vehicles, the manufacturer was able to tell the world that the reason was that the army left its vehicles in storage for a long time and that when the time came to put them on the road the soldiers overfilled them with oil. This is what might be called 'The Kipling Defence' – Tommy this and Tommy that and poor old Tommy who can't even read a dipstick taking the blame for pretty well everything – and is undoubtedly very useful to the manufacturer of *off-the-shelf* kit. 'Of course it's not soldier-proof,' he tells the ministry, 'but you have got what you paid for.'

The second is a neat example of what industry sees as the ungrateful attitude of the serviceman when he finds that his latest piece of equipment is not of the 'all-singing, all-dancing' variety. Already faced with a new *off-the-shelf* two-tonne truck which was by no means free of its teething troubles, one serviceman is reported as having said of the contest to select a new four-tonne cargo truck

> *'it doesn't matter what sort we get provided that there's room in the back for a two-tonner'.*

So the ministry has had to find what could be called a 'creative' way of satisfying its masters by bending the meaning of *off-the-shelf*. This is a variation on the car salesman's trick of persuading the customer to spend more money by ordering such 'optional extras' as electrically-operated sunshine roofs and central door-locking systems for his new car. All that the ministry has to do is to say to its order-hungry suppliers 'you can do this little bit extra for us can't you?' Thus it can ask for all sorts of extras – sometimes called *Non-Developmental Items* – but can still claim that because each was developed at the suppliers' expense, even the most exotic combinations are *off-the-shelf*. But it does not need very much to go wrong for the ministry to find itself enmeshed from head to toe in a web of self-deception.

Tucano – the Trainer That Taught Everybody a Lesson

In 1985 the ministry awarded a £132 million contract to Short Brothers of Belfast to build one-hundred-and-thirty Tucano basic trainer aircraft to replace the Royal Air Force's fleet of ageing Jet Provosts. It was the first major contract to be awarded under the ministry's newly introduced policy of tougher and more competitve procurement and, during the months following the announcement, Whitehall missed no opportunity to tell anybody who might have been even vaguely interested that a new day had dawned in the world of defence procurement. Tucano was an *off-the-shelf* design developed from an aircraft already in production in Brazil. Moreover, by choosing it, the ministry had lopped as much as £60 million from its original estimate of what the programme had been expected to cost and had been able to negotiate a firm price contract, which placed the entire responsibility for any cost overrun, no matter how caused, with Shorts.

What the ministry did not tell the world was, that when it had invited *best and final offers* in an effort to secure the best possible deal, it had *moved the goalposts* by increasing the speed requirement for its new trainer. Notwithstanding the late stage in the competition – it only had three weeks in which to make up its mind – Shorts decided that if it was to stay in the hunt it would have to fit a more powerful engine. To make things worse, Shorts seriously underestimated the amount of work that would be necessary to provide the *off-the-shelf* design with the 'extras' sought by the RAF, and the ministry, for its part, over-estimated Shorts' ability to manage the programme properly. With the 'extras' effectively reducing Tucano to only a twenty-two per cent *off-the-shelf* aircraft there was a dreadful inevitability about the outcome of the ministry's order. When Tucano eventually entered service it was generally reckoned to be a first-class aircraft. However it was late. By March 1989, when the RAF should have received fifty-nine aircraft, it had received only fifteen, the tax-payer was likely to be presented with a bill of £2.4 million for the cost of keeping the Jet Provosts flying, and Shorts had reported a loss of £47 million during 1988, part of which was almost certainly attributable to the difficulties with Tucano. Thus if the plane maker who was picking up the tab for the badly-managed project was to redeem its situation, somebody would almost certainly be asked to dig deeper into their pocket – and guess who owned Shorts at the time? Correct. Shorts belonged to the poor old British tax-payer.

One astonishing aspect of recent defence cock-ups is that very often when the men from the ministry come to the penitents' stool and are asked whether, at the time they awarded contracts, they had any doubts about the quality of the management of the contractors who have fallen down on the job, they are eventually compelled to reply 'Yes'. **The System** appears to have totally neglected Shorts' dismal financial record and an exchange of questions and answers during the parliamentary committee's enquiry into the Tucano affair provides a glimpse of the men from the ministry ducking and diving when they are put under pressure to explain their oversight.

When asked

> 'You knew that they had management problems and that their performance on the Javelin missile (no relation to the fighter described in Chapter Three) had been less than satisfactory'

the witness must have nodded because the chairman had to tell him that the shorthand writer could not record a nod. Having confirmed that he had replied in the affirmative the witness went on to tell the committee that

'The Ministry would have been aware of the position on the Javelin although myself I do not know what the position was at that time'.

A further comment by the chairman that the ministry must have known that Shorts had performed less than satisfactorily, drew the classic response

'If we had known what the situation was we would have been aware of it'.

That is not the sort of remark that anyone could take issue with, and even when the committee was able to establish that the ministry managed to get the ministry team to admit that it considered that the plane maker could handle the programme, Whitehall was able delicately to sidestep the Javelin missile's problems in the way that other pedestrians normally avoid upleasant messes on the sidewalk.

■
Keeping the Lid on Things

There was another attempt to find an *off-the-shelf* solution to a Royal Air Force requirement when the ministry unveiled plans for a £220 million programme to convert six Tristar airliners to serve as airborne tankers for refuelling its combat aircraft. The true cost of the project is still concealed beneath a row of asterisks in the official documents approved for publication. However some indication of the extent to which the programme has slipped into deep trouble may be found in the ministry's admission that it had not realised that each of the civilian aircraft that it had acquired for the purpose had been in effect 'hand-built' to a particular airline's specification and, therefore, presented an entirely different set of technical problems from its fellows.

Tucano is notable because it shows **The System**

trying to be too clever by half. Despite all the cries of injured innocence that echo down Whitehall at the very mention of the Ulster-built trainer it is difficult to imagine that there was not somebody somewhere, who said

'Well if they do get it wrong all they've got to do is...' or *'OK it's the tax-payer who pays but in this building we are £60 million to the good...so let's look around to see how we can spend it'.*

The Tristar muddle shows **The System** bumbling along trying to make do without enough people and just hoping everything will come right in the end. In its case it is hard to imagine that there was not somebody saying

'Well we'll just have to see how long we can keep the lid on this one'.

To which his colleagues might have replied *'Why not talk to the boys from Aldermaston, they're good at that sort of thing'.*

■

The Costliest Bomb of Them All

The boys from Aldermaston are very good indeed at keeping the lid on things. Since they are responsible for the production of the nation's stock of nuclear warheads, the ministry will not even say how many people work there. Probably the most notable of their cock-ups to have made the headlines was the mess they made in the early 1980s of controlling the costs of the Chevaline warhead for the Royal Navy's Polaris missile. The worrying thing about Aldermaston is that, despite being an establishment which designs and builds the most special of the special weapons, it seems to be none too good at getting its sums right. Take its estimates of the cost of building works in progress throughout the latter half of the 1980s at Aldermaston and its sister establishment Burghfield. This work was originally ordered to bring the facilities for handling and processing plutonium and radioactive wastes in line with health and safety requirements, and by 1985 the ministry thought they knew enough about what had to be done to be able to estimate that the cost would be in the region of £320 million.

Although the ministry was well aware of the scale of the cock-up on the cost of Chevaline, it seems to have had a touching faith, not only in Aldermaston's ability to run the works programme, but also to accept a massive burden of additional work involved in manufacturing the warheads for its newest Trident missiles and to bring the plant on-stream two years earlier than had originally been anticipated.

However the ministry was already in deep water and rapidly getting out of its depth. The Property Services Agency – over which the ministry has no jurisdiction except as a customer – had much of the responsibility for the works, and with time of the essence in the Trident programme, the call went out for tenders for much of the work before planning was complete and requirements properly established. The problems multiplied as it became clear that the PSA had to design and build structures without properly understanding the equipment which they were to house. Inevitably local management began to lose control. By 1986 the cost forecast had been recalculated to reveal that the works would cost at least £836 million and in the worst case as much as £1,069 million – of which the cost of the work on Trident itself was likely to be around only £50 million, but £657 million of the forecast cost related to projects that were not only critical to the missile programme but also beginning to fall badly behind schedule.

Trident was not a programme to be taken lightly. If the public got wind of a cock-up, the consequences in the form of Prime Ministerial wrath were too dreadful to contemplate. In the nick of time the ministry awarded a contract to one of the contractors who had managed complex projects in the North Sea oil and gas fields. Its brief at Aldermaston was to unscramble the contracts and clear the way for a management contractor who would eventually put in a team of more than 100 experts to keep the project on track.

Its most recent and most likely forecast of the total cost of the works is between £879 million and £1,133 million, a far cry from the £292 million which had been foreseen only seven years earlier.

◼

...and So it Goes On

Aldermaston illustrates the way in which the defence numbers have got bigger and continue to increase as **The Threat** becomes ever more complicated. Together with Tucano it also demonstrates the way in which the ministry has come to the realisation that it must combine a tougher approach to its contractors with better management of its own resources. Yet for all that, the problems which it faces today are, at their heart, no different from those which it didn't really notice as it continued to churn out useless Blackburn Bothas, when it really needed Spitfires. They are those associated with getting the right things to the right place at the right time. It probably did not really matter that the factory was making the wrong airplane at the wrong time, as there weren't enough of the right jigs at the right place at the right time for it to make anything else, anyhow. **The System** was satisfied with what was happening. At Aldermaston everything went right on the night, the management contractors did all the right things to keep the cost down and to keep the politicians off the civil servants' backs. **The System** is satisfied – it doesn't really matter that in the years when the project was running out of control there must have been quite a lot of civil servants saying

> *'Just look at these figures...we are going to have to push something to the right'.*

So it was, that because **The System** made it difficult for quite a lot of people to get their sums right, quite a lot of other people had to reappraise priorities that had been carefully related to **The Threat**. The chances are, that as they did so, they sowed the seeds of ... yet another cock-up.